CREATIVE BIBLE

MW00425612

Arts & Crafts

Karyn Henley

STANDARD
PUBLISHING
Cincinnati, Ohio

Cover design by B-LIN
Inside illustrations by Rusty Fletcher
Design and typography by Sherry F. Willbrand
Project editor, Ruth Frederick

The Standard Publishing Company, Cincinnati, Ohio
A division of Standex International Corporation

04   03   02   01   00   99   98   97   5   4   3   2   1

Library of Congress Cataloging-in-Publication Data

Henley, Karyn.
    Creative Bible learning/by Karyn Henley.
    p. cm.
    Includes index.
    Contents: [1] Arts & crafts — [3] Science & cooking — [3] Storytelling.
    ISBN 0-7847-0698-0 (v. 1). — ISBN 0-7847-0699-9 (v. 2). —
ISBN 0-7847-0697-2 (v. 3)
    1. Christian education of children. 2. Christian education—
Activity programs. 3. Bible crafts. I. Title.
    BV1475.2.H464   1997
    268'.432—dc21   97-6393
                                                                      CIP

Contents

Contents

Arts and Crafts

• Introduction •

Art activities make learning fun. A child can invest part of himself into art. He can use his imagination. He can explore the material he's working with. And he can learn about God at the same time.

This book is a guide that links art with Bible themes and stories. Use it two ways:
• In the index, locate the Bible story you will be teaching. With the story you will find a list of art activities that would be appropriate to use to supplement that story.
• In the table of contents, locate the art activity you want to do. When you turn to that activity in the book, you will find a list of Bible stories you could tell to give that art activity a spiritual emphasis.

Every activity also suggests questions to ask the children to encourage them to talk about the theme of the activity and/or review the story.

Both parents and children appreciate the chance to see the children's own artwork. So get ready for lots of smiles as you explore God's Word through art!

Paper

Straw Zoo

Materials
one piece of construction paper for each child
magazine pictures of zoo animals (already cut out)
glue
drinking straws

Guide Each Child To
1. Get one piece of construction paper and turn it horizontally.
2. Choose several pictures of animals.
3. Glue the pictures he chose onto his paper.
4. Glue straws across the paper to make zoo cage bars.

Talk About
- Who made animals?
- What is your favorite zoo animal?
- What sound does it make? How does it move around?
- What animal was in our story? Tell about it.

Suggested Bible Stories
Creation of Animals
Noah (animals)
Balaam's Talking Donkey
David, the Shepherd Boy
The Lost Sheep

Torn Tissue Fire

Materials
sheets of red, yellow, and orange tissue paper
one piece of heavy white paper or small white
    poster board for each child
one watercolor paintbrush for each child
plastic bowls
water
white glue
paper towels and water for clean-up

Guide Each Child To
1. Tear a medium-sized piece of each color of
tissue paper.
2. Set these three pieces on her white paper or
poster board to make them look like flames.
3. Mix equal amounts of water and glue in the
bowls. Stir with paintbrushes.
4. Dip her paintbrush into the glue mixture and
paint it over the tissue flames on the paper or
poster board.
5. Help clean her brush off with water and paper
towels.

Talk About
• Did you ever see a fire? Where?
• Why do we have to be careful with fire?
What are some things you can do to be
careful?
• Tell about the fire in our story.

Suggested Bible Stories
Burning Bush
Gideon
The Fiery Furnace
Jesus Makes Breakfast for His Friends

Envelope Butterflies

Materials

two envelopes of the same size for each child
scissors
crayons, markers
glue and glitter (optional)

Guide Each Child To

1. Cut off the flaps of each envelope.
2. Lick the midpoint of one flap and stick it to the midpoint of the other flap to make butterfly wings.
3. Decorate the wings with crayons, markers, glitter, and so on.

Talk About

• Have you ever seen a butterfly? What was it like?
• Who made butterflies?
• A butterfly is an insect. It has six legs. It has wings. What are some other insects God made?
• Tell about the animals in our story.
• For Easter: A caterpillar makes a cocoon. It stays inside for awhile and changes. When it comes out, it's a butterfly. When Jesus died, people put his body in a cave-like tomb. Did he stay there? What happened?

Suggested Bible Stories

Creation of Animals
Noah (animals)
The Resurrection

Halos

Materials

yellow construction paper or plain white paper cut into strips about ½ by 4 inches (about fifteen strips per child)
tape or stapler

Guide Each Child To

1. Form one strip of paper into a ring.
2. Tape or staple the ends together.
3. Loop the next strip of paper through the ring. Tape or staple its ends together.
4. Continue until the chain is long enough to fit onto his head comfortably.
5. Loop the last strip of paper through the rings on both ends of the chain to connect them. Tape or staple it to make a headband.

Talk About

• A long time ago, artists would paint halos above the heads of people and angels to show they were good. How can we show people today that we love God?
• What can people see in our lives that might make them want to be in God's kingdom?
• Who was the good person in our story? What did he choose to do that was right?
• What is something right and good that you can do?

Suggested Bible Stories

Solomon (dedicates the temple)
Singers Lead Jehoshaphat's Army
Gabriel Appears to Mary
Jesus Is Born
Angels Appear to the Shepherds
Jesus and the Children

Place Mats

Materials

two 18-inch lengths of waxed paper for each child
one construction paper heart for each child
iron
old towels
old crayons
crayon sharpener

Guide Each Child To

1. Lay one piece of waxed paper on folded towels.
2. Place the paper heart on top of the waxed paper.
3. Sharpen crayons of different colors so the shavings fall onto the waxed paper.
4. Place the other piece of waxed paper on top.
5. Watch as the teacher irons the place mat on a low heat setting to melt the crayon and waxed paper together.
6. Give her place mat to her mother or another special person.

Talk About

• What does it mean to *honor* someone? Is it always easy to honor others?
• Who was honored in our story? How did our character in the story show honor?
• Who will you give your place mat to?
• How do you feel when you get a gift? How do you feel when you give a gift?
• Why does God want us to be cheerful givers?
• Who gave a gift in our story?

Suggested Bible Stories

The Ten Commandments
Ruth
David and Jonathan
Abigail Packs Food
Queen of Sheba
Esther
Jesus as a Boy in the Temple
Two Sons and a Vineyard
The Widow's Mite

Tube Angels

Materials

cardboard tubes, about 6 inches in length, with two
   1-inch slits cut on opposite sides of the tube, 1
   inch down from the top
crayons, markers
plain white paper

Guide Each Child To

1. Color an angel face and robe on the tube.
2. Fold the paper accordion style.
3. Insert the folded paper into the tube through both slits.
4. Fan out the ends of the paper to make wings.

Talk About

- Who saw an angel in our story?
- What did the angel(s) do?
- Who sends angels? Why?

Suggested Bible Stories

Adam and Eve Leave the Garden
Jacob's Dream
Balaam's Talking Donkey
Daniel and the Lions
Gabriel Appears to Mary
John the Baptist Is Born
Joseph, Mary, and Jesus Move to Egypt
Jesus Goes Back to Heaven
Peter Escapes From Prison

paper in accordion-style fold

insert folded paper through both slits

Paper Hats

Materials
newspaper hats, folded as shown
construction paper stars and circles
scissors
crayons, markers

Guide Each Child To
1. Color her hat to look like the hat of a community helpers she has chosen.
2. Glue stars and circles on the hat to make the insignia of the community helper.

Talk About
- What kind of community helper would you like to be—a firefighter, police officer, or something else?
- How would you help people if you were a (suggest helpers)?
- Could you be a Christian and be a community helper too?
- God planned for us to have all kinds of friends. Who was the friend and helper in our story? How did he help?

Suggested Bible Stories
Joseph Leads Egypt
Jesus Chooses Twelve Friends (Peter was a fisherman, Matthew was a tax collector)
The Good Samaritan
Zacchaeus
Dorcas
Lydia

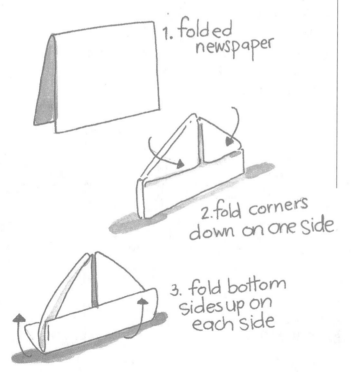

1. folded newspaper

2. fold corners down on one side

3. fold bottom sides up on each side

open out underneath for head to fit

Stuffed Fish

Materials
newspaper
small paper sacks
crayons, markers
string

Guide Each Child To
1. Stuff a small paper sack with wadded newspaper until it is halfway full.
2. Help the teacher gather the sack at the opening and tie it with string. The tied end becomes the tail of the fish.
3. Draw the fish's eyes, fins, and mouth on the stuffed end.

Talk About
• Where do fish live? What other creatures live in the water?
• Have you ever gone fishing? Where?
• If anyone was out fishing on the day of our story, what would they have seen?

Suggested Bible Stories
Creation of Animals
Jonah
Jesus Chooses Twelve Friends (the fishermen)
The Great Catch of Fish
Jesus Feeds 5,000
The Fish and the Net
Tax Money in a Fish
Jesus Makes Breakfast for His Friends

Shape Creatures

Materials
construction paper, all colors, cut in a variety of geometrical shapes
glue
crayons, markers

Guide Each Child To
1. Arrange the shapes you have given him to form an animal.
2. Glue these shapes onto his paper.
3. Use crayons and markers to draw features on his animal.

IDEAS: Use the paper shapes to make flowers and trees for Creation or the Sermon on the Mount. Make vehicles for the story of Abraham's move, Ruth's travels, or the Israelites traveling to the promised land.

Talk About
• Who made animals? What is your favorite animal?
• Do you have any animals that live at your house?
• What makes people different from animals?
• Name some animals and tell how they move. Tell how they sound.
• What kinds of animals were in our story? What happened?

Suggested Bible Stories
Creation of Animals
Adam Names the Animals
Noah (animals)
Balaam's Talking Donkey
David, the Shepherd Boy
Daniel and the Lions
Jonah
Jesus Is Born
The Triumphal Entry

Stained Glass Star

Materials
plain white paper
black marker
crayons
baby oil
cotton balls
magazines

Guide Each Child To
1. Use the black marker to draw a simple star on the piece of paper.
2. Color the entire page using crayons.
3. Create "stained glass" sections by adding more lines to make new areas of color around the star.
4. Lay the paper on a magazine and get a cotton ball that has baby oil on it. Rub the oil over the paper, making it translucent.
5. Hold the paper up to the light or tape it to a window so the light will shine through it.

IDEAS: This "stained glass" window can be used for other lessons by changing the picture in it. For example, write the word JOY or LOVE and let the children color in the letters. Or draw a flower for a lesson on "Consider the Lilies." Draw a sun for a lesson on how the sun stood still.

Talk About
- What do you see in the sky at night?
- Who made the moon and the stars?
- Who saw the stars (or the moon) in our story?
- What did the star in our story mean?

Suggested Bible Stories
Creation of Sun, Moon, and Stars
God's Promise to Abraham
Joseph's Dreams
The Wise Men

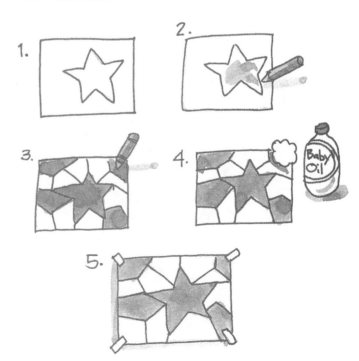

Funny Faces

Materials

construction paper
magazines
scissors
glue

Guide Each Child To

1. Cut out facial features from magazines—eyes from one picture, ears from another, mouth from another, and so on.
2. Glue them onto the construction paper to make a completely new face.

Talk About

• Who is the only one who can create a real person?
• What color is your skin? What color are your eyes? What color are the eyes on the pictures you made?
• What color is your hair? What color is the hair on the pictures you made?
• How is everyone alike? How is everyone different? Who made us that way?
• Who was the special person in our story? How did God help him?

Suggested Bible Stories

Creation of People
Naaman
Through the Roof
The Lame Man at the Pool
The Centurion's Sick Servant
Woman Touches Jesus' Hem
Jairus's Daughter
Blind Bartimaeus
Zacchaeus
Peter and John Heal a Lame Man

Two Hearts

Materials
plain white paper (8½ by 11 inches)
colored paper cut in 8½-by-5½-inch pieces
scissors
glue

Guide Each Child To
1. Fold the colored paper in half.
2. Let the teacher draw half of a heart shape on the fold as shown.
3. Cut a heart from the colored paper by cutting where the teacher has drawn. (Some children may need help with this.)
4. Glue the colored paper with the heart cut out onto one half of the plain white paper.
5. Glue the colored heart on the other half of the plain white paper as shown.

Talk About
- What does a heart make you think of?
- Who showed love in our story? How did they show love?
- How does God show his love for you?
- How can you show God's love to other people?

Suggested Bible Stories
Jacob's Family (Jacob and Rachel)
Ruth
David and Jonathan
Jesus Is Born
The Crucifixion

Heart Fans

Materials

construction paper cut into 8-inch hearts
(Write "Love the Lord with all your heart and soul and mind" on the front. Write "Love your neighbor as yourself" on the back.)
drinking straws
crayons, markers
tape

Guide Each Child To

1. Color a border around the edges of the heart, front and back.
2. Tape a drinking straw to the heart to make a handle.
3. Use the heart as a fan.

Talk About

• How can you love God with all your heart, soul, and mind?
• Who is your neighbor?
• Can you love yourself? How? How can you love your neighbor as yourself?
• Who showed love in our story? How?

Suggested Bible Stories

Ruth
David and Jonathan
Jesus Is Born
The Good Samaritan
Jesus Washes His Friends' Feet
The Crucifixion

Helmets

Materials
poster board cut lengthwise, half sheet per child
crayons, markers
stapler
colored tissue paper

Guide Each Child To
1. Let the teacher curve the poster board around his head, as shown. It should fit snugly, but not too tightly. Staple to fit.
2. Let the teacher mark and cut eye slits as shown.
3. Staple tissue paper on the rim to flow out like a feather.
4. Color the helmet.

Talk About
• What is a helmet for?
• What are some other things a Bible times soldier might have worn in a fight?

Suggested Bible Stories
Gideon
David and Goliath
Servant Sees God's Army
The Centurion's Sick Servant
The Resurrection (soldiers at the tomb)
Spiritual Armor

New Ears

Materials
sheets of construction paper
cardboard or construction paper, cut into 1-inch-
   wide strips
scissors
stapler
crayons, markers

Guide Each Child To
1. Let the teacher staple or tape strips together
until they fit around the child's head like a crown.
2. Draw large ears, any kind (silly, animal) on a
sheet of construction paper.
3. Color the ears and cut them out.
4. Attach the ears to the headband to wear. Ears
can stick up, hang down or be folded to point out
to the sides.

Talk About
• Who made your ears?
• What are some sounds you like to hear?
What are some sounds you don't like to hear?
• Who listened in our story? What did she
hear?

Suggested Bible Stories
Birthright and Blessing
Samuel Hears God
The Wise Man's House
Mary and Martha
Blind Bartimaeus
Paul's Nephew Hears a Plot

Blessing Wall Hanging

Materials

3-by-5-inch index cards (six cards for each child—
   three blank and three with one word written on
   each: BLESS, THIS, HOUSE)
crayons, markers
ribbon
stapler
scissors

Guide Each Child To

1. Color designs on her cards.
2. Lay out a long piece of ribbon vertically.
3. Help the teacher staple the card that says
BLESS and a blank card back-to-back, one
fourth of the way down the ribbon.
4. Help staple the card that says *THIS* and a blank
card back-to-back, halfway down the ribbon.
5. Staple the card that says *HOUSE* back-to-back,
three fourths of the way down the ribbon.

Talk About

• To *bless* your house means to pray that
God will bring good things to your house and
the people who live there. Who lives at your
house?
• How has God blessed you and the people
at your house?
• Who lived at the house in our story? What
happened there?

Suggested Bible Stories

Rahab and the Spies
Peter's Mother-in-Law
Through the Roof
Jairus's Daughter
The Wise Man's House

Envelope Animals

Materials
monarch envelopes (cut as shown)
crayons, markers
transparent tape
cotton balls, glue (for sheep)

Guide Each Child To
1. Fold up the two sides of the animal's neck as shown.
2. Color the animal. Depending on the story, the animal can be a donkey, a horse, a zebra, or other animal that might have been on Noah's ark.
3. Tape the two sides of the head together at the top, and tape the neck to the body.
4. For a sheep: Glue cotton balls on the animal and fold the ears down.
5. Stand the animal up by spreading the legs.

Talk About
- Who made animals?
- What kind of animal was in our story? What happened?
- What is your favorite animal?

Suggested Bible Stories
Creation of Animals
Noah (animals)
Abraham Travels
Saul Looks for Lost Donkeys
David, the Shepherd Boy
Elijah Goes to Heaven
Jesus Is Born
Angels Appear to the Shepherds
The Lost Sheep
The Triumphal Entry

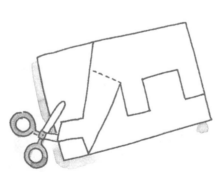
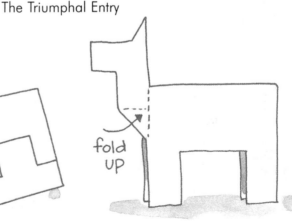

fold up

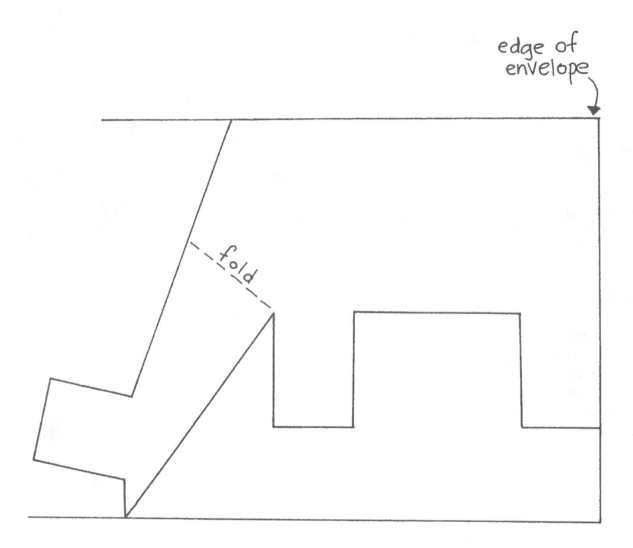

edge of
envelope

fold

Paper Sailboats

Materials
plain white paper cut into triangles with a 4-inch base and 5-inch sides
plastic picnic bowls
toothpicks
modeling dough (see recipes, pages 116-121)
a sink or tub of water (optional)

Guide Each Child To
1. Color the paper sail for his boat.
2. Place a piece of modeling dough or clay in the center of the bowl.
3. Tape a toothpick to the back of the sail at the base so the toothpick sticks out.
4. Stick the toothpick into the dough or clay in the bowl so the sail stands up.
5. Sail his boat in water.

Talk About
• Did you ever go sailing in a boat? If you did, what was it like?
• Who went sailing in our story? What happened?
• How did God help the people in our story?
• How does God help you?

Suggested Bible Stories
Noah (boats)
Jonah
The Great Catch of Fish
Jesus Stills the Storm
Jesus Walks on Water
Paul's Shipwreck

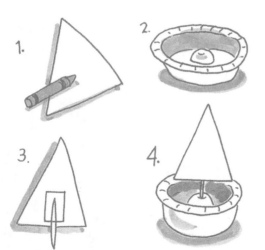

Heart Necklace

Materials
red poster-board hearts (pattern on page 28)
hole punch
string or yarn cut into 14-inch lengths
uncooked, hollow cylindrical pasta (ziti or rigatoni)

Guide Each Child To
1. Punch a hole in the top of the heart.
2. Put the string or yarn through the hole in the heart. Then add pasta to the string on both sides of the heart.
3. Let the teacher tie the ends of the string or yarn so that the necklace fits loosely around the child's neck.

Talk About
• What do we have to be thankful for?
• How can we show our thankfulness to God? When? Where?
• How can we show love?
• Who showed love in our story?

Suggested Bible Stories
Isaac Is Born
Ruth
Jesus Is Born
Water Into Wine
The Good Samaritan
The Runaway Son
Ten Lepers
Zacchaeus
The Crucifixion

Paint

Crumpled Paper Print Clouds

Materials
one piece of blue construction paper for each child
white tempera paint
paper plates
old newspapers

Guide Each Child To
1. Tear a sheet of newspaper in half and crumple it up tightly.
2. Cover the bottom of the paper plates with paint.
3. Holding one side of the crumpled paper, press the paper ball into the paint and then onto the blue paper. The blue paper is the sky, and the white prints are the clouds.

Talk About
• What are clouds made of? Who made clouds?
• What comes out of a gray cloudy sky?
• What happened with the weather or clouds in our story?

Suggested Bible Stories
Noah
The Cloud Covers the Tabernacle
Elijah on Mt. Carmel (servant sees a cloud)
Jesus Stills the Storm
Jesus Goes Back to Heaven
Paul's Shipwreck

Flower Prints

Materials
artificial flowers (carnation-type flowers work best)
paper
paper plates
a variety of colors of paint

Guide Each Child To
1. Help pour a little paint onto each plate to just cover the bottom of the plate. Use one plate for each color of paint.
2. Dip the flower into the paint.
3. Press the flower onto the paper to make a print.
4. Make several prints of various colors.

Talk About
• Have you ever seen a flower garden? What was it like?
• Who made flowers?
• What is your favorite kind of flower?
• Tell about the garden in our story. What happened?

Suggested Bible Stories
Creation of Plants
Garden of Eden
Aaron's Staff Blooms
Birds and Flowers (Sermon on the Mount)
The Resurrection (garden tomb)

Thumbprint Flowers

Materials
box of watercolors (dampened)
paintbrush
cup of water
smocks
plain white paper
crayons, markers
paper towels or moist towelettes

Guide Each Child To
1. Draw lines from the middle of her paper to the bottom.
2. Press her thumb gently onto the damp paint and then press several times around the top of one of her lines to make a flower.
3. Repeat the process with different colors for the different lines.
4. Clean her hands on damp paper towels.

Talk About
• Your thumbprint is very special. No one else in the world has a thumbprint that looks like yours. Who gave you such a special thumbprint?
• Who made people? Did he like the way he made them?
• Are all people different? How are people alike?
• Tell about the flowers or garden in our story. Who made flowers?

Suggested Bible Stories
Creation of Plants, People
Garden of Eden
Aaron's Staff Blooms
Birds and Flowers (Sermon on the Mount)
The Resurrection (garden tomb)

String Painting

Materials

smocks
paper towels
bowls for each color of paint
several pieces of string about 8 inches long
newspaper
tempera paint
paper

Guide Each Child To

1. Help cover the work area with newspaper.
2. Help pour paint into the bowls.
3. Dip a piece of string into the paint.
4. Lay the string on the paper, with one end of the string (the end without paint on it) hanging off the paper.
5. Fold the paper over the string.
6. While pressing down on the string and paper with one hand, pull the string out with the other hand.
7. Open the paper to see the design.
8. Repeat with other colors of paint, if you wish.

Talk About
• What does your painting make you think of?
• The blue reminds me of rain. Who made rain? When it rains for a long time, what happens?
• What do we call the kind of weather that rains and thunders and makes lightning?
• What else might be part of a storm?
• Who takes care of you during a storm?

Suggested Bible Stories
Creation of Sky, Sea, and Land
Noah (flood)
Elijah on Mount Carmel (servant sees a cloud)
Jonah
Jesus Stills the Storm
The Wise Man's House
Paul's Shipwreck

Straw Blown Tree

Materials
paper
thin brown or black watercolor paint
eye dropper or spoon
drinking straws
newspaper
paper towels

Guide Each Child To
1. Help cover the work area with newspaper.
2. Let the teacher drop a small amount of paint onto her paper.
3. Blow through the straw onto the paint. The paint will "branch out" in lines as it spreads, making a tree shape.

Talk About
• Can you name some of the parts of a tree?
• What is a tree good for?
• Who made trees?
• Tell me about the tree in our story.
• Do you have lots of trees in your yard at home?
• What do we call a place that has lots and lots of trees?

Suggested Bible Stories
Creation of Plants
Adam and Eve Eat the Fruit
Burning Bush
Deborah
Jonah (and the vine)
Zacchaeus

Sponge Painted Night

Materials

newspaper

manila paper

sponges cut in 2-inch squares, with a clothespin clipped to each for a handle

black and blue paint

disposable pie plates

paper towels

smocks

optional: yellow construction paper moon and star shapes; glue

Guide Each Child To

1. Help cover the work area with newspaper.
2. Help pour enough black paint in one pie plate to cover the bottom of the plate.
3. Help pour the same amount of blue paint in another pie plate.
4. Press a sponge into the paint, then press it gently onto the paper as if stamping.
5. Fill the paper with black and blue prints.
6. Glue moon and stars onto the page, if desired.

Talk About

- Who made the night?
- What is in the sky at night?
- Are some nights darker than others? Why?
- What do you like about night?
- Can you think of any animals that do their work at night?
- What happened at night in our story?

Suggested Bible Stories

Creation of Sun, Moon, and Stars

Jacob's Dream

Joseph's Dreams

The Plagues in Egypt (darkness, firstborn)

Gideon

Samson (taking the gates)

Samuel Hears God

David Spares Saul's Life at Night

Angels Appear to the Shepherds

The Wise Men

Nicodemus Visits Jesus at Night

The Crucifixion (darkness over the land)

Marble Painting

Materials
paper
shallow box that the paper will fit in
marbles, small balls, or round Christmas ornaments
paint
paper towels
smocks

Guide Each Child To
1. Help cover the work area with newspaper.
2. Help pour paint into bowls.
3. Place the paper in the shallow box.
4. Dip the marble, ball, or ornament into the paint. Set it on the paper. Scoot and shake the box back and forth to make the ball roll across the paper several times, leaving a trail of paint.

Talk About
• What is your favorite color? Who made colors?
• These lines make me think of roads. If this painting were a map, where would you want these roads to go?
• Where did the road in our story go? Who went on the road? How did they travel?

Suggested Bible Stories
Abraham Travels
Joseph Is Taken to Egypt
Joseph's Brothers Go To Egypt
The Israelites Wander in the Wilderness
Balaam's Talking Donkey
Ruth
Joseph, Mary, and Jesus Move to Egypt
Jesus as a Boy in the Temple
The Good Samaritan
The Runaway Son
The Triumphal Entry
Philip and the Man From Ethiopia
Paul to Damascus

Salt Painting

Materials
construction paper
salt mixed with red, yellow, and blue powdered
   tempera paint, each color in a different cup
large shallow box

Guide Each Child To
1. Place construction paper in the box.
2. Put glue on the paper, then sprinkle the salt-paint on the glue.
3. Shake the excess off into the box.

Talk About
• What colors do you see? Who made colors?
• What can you think of that is red? What is blue? What is yellow?
• Let's thank God for making colors. Can we thank God anytime? Anywhere? How do we thank him?

Suggested Bible Stories
Creation of Light and Color
Noah (rainbows)
Joseph's Colorful Coat
Ten Lepers

Crayon Resist Storm

Materials
manila paper
crayons
watercolors
paintbrushes
cups of water
paper towels
smocks

Guide Each Child To
1. Color a boat and lightning on manila paper, pressing down very hard with the crayon to build up the wax on the paper.
2. Paint over the boat and lightning with the watercolors to make a storm. The waxy crayon drawing will resist the paint, and the boat and lightning will show through.

Talk About
• What is a storm?
• Who was in the storm in our story? What was happening to him? How do you think he felt? Who took care of him?
• Have you ever been outside in a storm? How would you feel?
• Who takes care of us in a storm?

Suggested Bible Stories
Noah (flood)
The Plagues in Egypt (color white hail that will show when painted over)
Elijah on Mt. Carmel (color fire from heaven and altar)
Jonah
Jesus Stills the Storm
The Wise Man's House
Paul's Shipwreck

Toy Car Painting

Materials

plastic toy cars (or buses, truck, trains)
manila paper
variety of colors of paint (finger paint or tempera)
paper towels
smocks
newspaper
paper plates

Guide Each Child To

1. Help cover the work area with newspaper.
2. Help pour a small amount of paint on a paper plate, one plate per color of paint.
3. Dip the wheels of a toy car into the paint.
4. Roll the car wheels over the manila paper to make tracks.

Talk About

• Do you ever take a trip in your car? Where do you like to go?
• How else could you travel? Would God go with you? How do you know?
• Who took a trip in our story? How did they travel?

Suggested Bible Stories

Abraham Travels
Joseph Is Taken to Egypt
Joseph's Brothers Go to Egypt
The Israelites Wander in the Wilderness
Naaman
Joseph, Mary, and Jesus Move to Egypt
Jesus as a Boy in the Temple
The Good Samaritan
The Runaway Son
The Triumphal Entry
Philip and the Man From Ethiopia
Paul to Damascus

Bubble Pop Picture

Materials
bubble blowing soap
paper bowls
bubble blowing wands
liquid tempera paint in bright, bold colors
plain white paper
newspaper

Guide Each Child To
1. Go outdoors for this activity or cover the table with newspaper.
2. Mix a few drops of paint with the bubble soap in bowls, using a different bowl for each color.
3. Let the teacher blow colored bubbles over the newspaper or outdoors over the grass.
4. Try to catch the bubbles on the paper and let them pop on the paper, making a design.

Hint: Let the children practice moving in slow motion before starting this activity. They will catch more bubbles by moving slowly and letting the bubbles fall onto their papers.

Talk About
- Who made colors?
- What is your favorite color?
- What was colorful in our story?
- What happened in our story?

Suggested Bible Stories
Creation of Light and Color
Noah (rainbows)
Joseph's Colorful Coat

Pudding Painting

Materials
instant pudding of any flavor
milk
paper bowls or cups
large bowl and spoon
liquid measuring cup
shelf paper or finger paint paper
paper towels

Guide Each Child To
1. Help cover the work area with newspaper.
2. Wash hands.
3. Mix the pudding according to package directions.
4. Put a little pudding in small paper bowls or cups.
5. Finger-paint on the paper with the pudding, tasting the "paint" if he desires.
6. Wash hands afterwards.

Talk About
• This is a pudding painting. You may taste it. How does it taste? Is it sour, salty, sweet, or bitter?
• What is flavor? Who planned for foods to have flavor?
• What part of your body tastes flavor? What kind of food was in our story? Who ate it?

Suggested Bible Stories
Adam and Eve Eat the Fruit
Abraham and the Three Visitors
Birthright and Blessing
Manna and Quail
Ruth
Ravens Feed Elijah
A Widow Shares With Elijah
Daniel Refuses the King's Food
John the Baptist (locusts and honey)
Jesus Feeds 5,000
The Runaway Son
Jesus Makes Breakfast for His Friends

Chalk Sunset

Materials
buttermilk
paper cups
colored chalk
paper
smocks

Guide Each Child To
1. Dip the chalk in buttermilk.
2. Rub the chalk across the paper to paint a sunset.

Talk About
• Have you ever seen a sunset? What colors did you see in the sky? How did the clouds look? How did the sun look?
• At what time of day can you see a sunset? Have you seen a sunrise? What does it look like?
• Who keeps the sun rising and setting?

Suggested Bible Stories
Creation of Sun, Moon, and Stars
The Sun Stands Still
Let Your Light Shine (Sermon on the Mount)
John Sees Heaven

Cup Print

Materials

plastic communion cups
paper plates or pie tins
purple tempera paint
manila paper
paper towels

Guide Each Child To

1. Help cover the bottom of the paper plates or pie tins with the paint.
2. Turn her cup upside down and dip the rim of it into the paint.
3. Print it onto the paper, making a purple circle.
4. Repeat the process until she has printed a "bunch" of grapes.

Talk About
- Where does grape juice come from?
- Who had a vineyard in our story, or who drank the juice from the grapes?
- What happened?

Suggested Bible Stories
Baker, Cupbearer, and Pharaoh's Dreams
   (cupbearer's dream)
Twelve Spies
Nehemiah, the King's Cupbearer
Water Into Wine
Two Sons and a Vineyard
The Lord's Supper

Cotton Swab Painting

Materials
paper
cotton swabs
watercolor paints
   (keep damp throughout the activity)
paper towels
newspaper

Guide Each Child To
1. Help cover the work area with newspaper.
2. Dab his cotton swab in the dampened watercolors and paint a picture on his paper.

Talk About
• You are working hard to make a beautiful picture. Who worked hard in our story? What happened?
• What kind of work do you do at home?
• What kind of work do you do in your classroom?

Suggested Bible Stories
Noah (boat)
Tower of Babel
Joseph Leads Egypt
Deborah
Ruth
David, the Shepherd Boy
A Widow's Oil Jars
King Josiah Finds God's Word
Rebuilding Jerusalem's Walls
Two Sons and a Vineyard

Shave Cream Clouds

Materials

cans of shaving cream
large pieces of light blue construction paper
watercolor paints

Guide Each Child To

1. Spray several dollops of shave cream onto her paper.
2. With fingers, spread these clouds across the paper sky.
3. Add drips of different colors of watercolor paint to the clouds and swirl them around.

Talk About

• What did God put up in the sky?
• What happens to the clouds at sunrise and sunset?
• What do the clouds look like on a rainy day?
• What did the clouds do in our story? What happened?

Suggested Bible Stories

Creation of Sky, Sea, and Land
Noah (flood)
The Ten Commandments (Moses on Mt. Sinai)
The Cloud Covers the Tabernacle
Elijah on Mt. Carmel (servant sees a cloud)
Jonah (weather)
Jesus Stills the Storm
Jesus Walks on Water
Jesus Goes Back to Heaven
John Sees Heaven

Shoe Prints

Materials
old shoes or beach sandals of different sizes with
fairly clean soles
manila paper
tempera paints
9-by-13-inch cake pan or shirt box
newspaper
paper towels
smocks

Guide Each Child To
1. Help cover the work area with newspaper.
2. Help cover the bottom of the cake pan or shirt
box with paint.
3. Press the sole of the shoe into the paint and
then onto the paper.
4. Make prints of different shoe sizes on her paper.

Talk About
• Who in your family wears shoes that are
this size? Who is the biggest person in your
family? Who is the smallest?
• Who was the father in the family in our
story? Who was the mother? Who were the
children?
• Who planned for us to have families? Why
do we need families?

Suggested Bible Stories
Adam and Eve Have a Family
Noah (family)
Isaac Is Born
Jacob and Esau
Jacob's Family
Baby Moses
David Is Anointed
The Runaway Son

Moon Prints

Materials
dark blue or purple paper
yellow finger paint
newspaper
smocks
paper towels

Guide Each Child To
1. Help cover the work area with newspaper.
2. Stretch out his hand, fingers and thumb together; then curve his hand.
3. Place the side of his hand into the paint and then onto the paper, making crescent moons.

curved hand to make a print

Talk About
• Sometimes the moon is big and round, and sometimes it has a crescent shape like this. What else is in the nighttime sky?
• What do you like about nighttime?
• What does God do while you are asleep?
• How did God take care of the person in our story?

Suggested Bible Stories
Creation of Sun, Moon, and Stars
Joseph's Dreams
Gideon
Samson (taking the gates)
Samuel Hears God
David Spares Saul's Life at Night
Nicodemus Visits Jesus at Night
Jesus in Gethsemane
Paul in a Basket

Sponge Print Crosses

Materials
sponges cut into cross shapes
disposable pie plates
paper
newspaper
smocks
paint
paper towels

Guide Each Child To
1. Help cover the work area with newspaper.
2. Press the sponge into a paint pan, then press the sponge onto her paper several times.
3. Make the cross prints side-by-side.

Talk About
• What does the cross shape make us think about?
• Why did God send his Son, Jesus, to the earth?
• Why did Jesus die on the cross?
• Did Jesus stay dead? Where is Jesus now?

Suggested Bible Story
The Crucifixion

Drawing

Footprint People

Materials
one large piece of paper for each child
pencils or pens
crayons, markers

Guide Each Child To
1. Take off his shoes and socks. (If he doesn't want to remove socks and shoes, let him do this activity with socks and shoes on.)
2. Stand on a piece of paper.
3. Trace around his feet.
4. Draw features inside the foot so that it looks like a funny foot person.

Talk About
• Who made you? Who made your feet?
• Do you like to wear shoes on your feet, or would you rather go barefoot? What kind of shoes are your favorite?
• Could the feet in our story walk?
• What happened to the feet in our story?

Suggested Bible Stories
Creation of People
David and Mephibosheth
Through the Roof
The Lame Man at the Pool
Perfume on Jesus' Feet
Jesus Washes His Friends' Feet
Peter and John Heal a Lame Man

Hand Trees

Materials

large pieces of manila paper or butcher paper
crayons, markers

Guide Each Child To

1. Let the teacher trace over her hands, fingers
spread, to make four handprints with part of her
arms, as shown.
2. Color one handprint brown, like a bare tree.
3. Color flowers on the next tree.
4. Color the next tree with green leaves all over it.
5. Color the last tree with gold and orange leaves.

Talk About

• Which tree looks like a wintertime tree?
Which looks like spring? Which looks like
summer? Which looks like autumn or fall?
Which season is the season that God is with
us? He's with us all the time!
• Who made trees? What are trees used for?
• Do you have trees in your yard? Are all
trees alike? How are they different?
• Name some parts of a tree.
• What kinds of food do we eat that come
from trees?

Suggested Bible Stories

Creation of Plants
Adam and Eve Eat the Fruit
Noah (the dove brings back an olive leaf)
Burning Bush
Deborah
Zacchaeus

Ring Mural

Materials
crayons
butcher paper

Guide Each Child To
1. Let the teacher draw a circle for each child that interlocks with a circle of the child next to him.
2. Use a color of crayon that will blend to make a new color when it's put on top of the color in the next circle. (For example: the first child has yellow. She colors her circle yellow. Then the next child colors his circle blue. Where the first two circles overlap, that area will be green. Give the next child red, the next yellow, then blue, red, yellow, and so on.)
3. Color the inside of his circle.

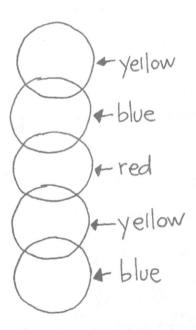

Talk About
• When we share with friends, special things happen. What can you share? Can you share a space on paper?
• Who planned for us to be friends and have friends?
• Who were the friends in the story? Was the friend a good friend or a bad friend? What happened?

Suggested Bible Stories
Abraham and the Three Visitors
David and Jonathan
A Widow Shares With Elijah
Elisha's Room on the Roof
Daniel Refuses the King's Food
The Fiery Furnace
The Wise Men
Jesus Chooses Twelve Friends
Through the Roof
Mary and Martha
Jesus Washes His Friends' Feet
Paul and Silas in Prison

Kind Hands Mural

Materials
construction paper
crayons, markers
scissors
butcher paper
glue or tape

Guide Each Child To
1. Trace around his hand on construction paper.
2. Cut out his hand tracing. (Some children may need help with this.)
3. Write his name or let the teacher help him write his name on his paper hand.
4. Glue or tape the hands onto the butcher paper to make a circle, with the hands touching.
5. Write at the bottom of the mural, "Be kind to one another."

Talk About
- How can we be kind to others?
- Is it always easy to be kind?
- How can your hands show kindness? How can your mouth show kindness? How can your ears show kindness? How can your feet show kindness?
- Who was kind in our story?

Suggested Bible Stories
Abraham and the Three Visitors
Rahab and the Spies
Ruth
David and Jonathan
A Widow Shares With Elijah
Elisha's Room on the Roof
Through the Roof
The Good Samaritan
Jesus and the Children
Jesus Washes His Friends' Feet

Neighborhood Map

Materials
blocks
butcher paper
crayons, markers
toy cars, buses, trucks

Guide Each Child To
1. Draw a neighborhood street map on butcher paper.
2. Place blocks along the street for houses and business buildings.
3. Draw grass, flowers, and so on.
4. Roll the cars, buses, and trucks down the streets of the map.

Talk About
• What do we call people who live next to us and down the street?
• Can neighbors be friends? Do you have friends who live in your neighborhood? Do you have friends who live other places?
• Why are they your friends? What is a friend?
• Can God be your friend? How do you talk to God?
• Who were the friends in our story? What happened?

Suggested Bible Stories
Ruth
David and Jonathan
Elisha's Room on the Roof
Daniel Refuses the King's Food
The Fiery Furnace
Jesus Chooses Twelve Friends
The Good Samaritan
Mary and Martha
Paul and Silas in Prison

Coin Rubbings

Materials
coins
paper
crayons

Guide Each Child To
1. Place the coins under her paper.
2. Rub over the paper with the side of the crayon. The coin design will show through.

Talk About
- What coins do you see?
- God gives us everything. How does he give us money? What could we do with our money to use it wisely?
- Who had money in our story? What happened?

Suggested Bible Stories
Joseph's Brothers Go to Egypt (to buy grain)
The Lost Coin
Zacchaeus
The Widow's Mite
Tax Money in a Fish

Profiles

Materials

large sheets of manila paper
crayons, markers

Guide Each Child To

1. Lay his head down sideways on the paper.
2. Let the teacher draw around his head to make a profile of him.
3. Draw inside the profile things he is thankful for.

Talk About

• What are you thankful for? How do you show that you are thankful?
• Whom do we thank? Why do we say thank-you?
• Who was thankful in our story?
• How are you like everyone else? How are you different?
• What kinds of things do you like?
• What was the person in our story like?

Suggested Bible Stories

Thankfulness:
Anna and Simeon
Ten Lepers

God Made Us All Different:
Jacob and Esau
Samson
The Woman at the Well
Jesus and the Children
Zacchaeus

Surprise Picture

Materials

crayons

cardboard angel shapes glued onto construction paper, covered with plain white paper so the shapes are "sandwiched" between (one for each child)

Guide Each Child To

Color over the white paper. As he does, the shapes underneath show up as "rubbings."

Talk About
• What did the angel in the story do? How did the person in the story act when he saw the angel?
• Whose message did the angel bring to earth?

Suggested Bible Stories

Adam and Eve Leave the Garden
Jacob's Dream
Balaam's Talking Donkey
Samson (an angel tells of Samson's birth)
Daniel and the Lions
Gabriel Appears to Mary
John the Baptist Is Born
Angels Appear to the Shepherds
The Resurrection (angels at the empty tomb)
Jesus Goes Back to Heaven
Peter Escapes From Prison

Hand Lions

Materials

plain white paper

crayons

Guide Each Child To

1. Put her hand on the paper with her fingers spread out.
2. Let the teacher trace around her hand onto the plain white paper.
3. Turn the paper around and place her hand on the paper again, palm to palm, so that her fingers are pointing the opposite way from the fingers that were just drawn.
4. Let the teacher trace around her hand again. The fingers on the drawing become the lion's mane.
5. Draw a lion's face in the center of the mane.
6. Color in the face and the mane.

Talk About
- Who saw a lion in our story? What happened?
- Who was taking care of the person in our story?
- Who takes care of you?
- How does God take care of you?

Suggested Bible Stories

Creation of Animals

Noah (animals)

Samson (kills a lion)

David, the Shepherd Boy

Daniel and the Lions

Growing Flowers

Materials

large pieces of construction paper cut in half length-wise, folded in approxmately four 2-inch accordion-style folds

crayons

seeds

glue

Guide Each Child To

1. Draw the petals of a flower on the top fold.
2. Glue a seed on the bottom fold.
3. Draw the stem and leaves from the seed up to the petals. The flower will "grow" as it is unfolded.

Talk About

- What can grow besides people?
- What is the difference between plants and people? Can plants grow in wisdom? Can animals grow in wisdom?
- Who planned for plants to grow?
- What plant was in our story? What happened?
- Who grew in our story? What happened?

Suggested Bible Stories

Plants:

Creation of Plants

Baby Moses (hidden in the reeds)

Burning Bush

Jonah (and the vine)

Growing:

Adam and Eve Have a Family

Isaac Is Born

Jacob and Esau

Joseph's Dreams

Baby Moses

Samuel's New Coats

David, the Shepherd Boy

Joash, Boy King

Josiah, Boy King

Jesus as a Boy in the Temple

Bandannas

Materials
18-inch squares of light, solid-colored cloth
fabric markers
newspaper

Guide Each Child To
1. Help spread newspaper over the tables or floor.
2. Place the cloth on top of the newspaper.
3. Draw colorful designs on the cloth to make a bandanna.
4. Decide how he wants to wear his bandanna.

Talk About
• Who planned for us to have clothes to wear?
• Did anyone ever sew clothes for you? How did they do it?
• What is your favorite thing to wear?
• What kind of clothes did the person in our story make or wear?

Suggested Bible Stories
Joseph's Colorful Coat
Samuel's New Coats
Dorcas

Add-On Drawings

Materials

paper with a circle drawn on it for the head of a
  figure
crayons, markers

Guide Each Child To

1. Write her name on the back of her paper.
2. Draw two eyes on the circle and give the paper to the person next to her.
3. Add a mouth and pass the paper to the next person.
4. Add a nose and pass the paper again.
5. Continue in this way adding ears, hair, neck, body, and so on, until the papers get back to their original owners.

Talk About

• You shared. What does God think about sharing?
• How does it make other people feel when you share with them?
• Who shared in our story? What did they share?

Suggested Bible Stories

Abraham and the Three Visitors
David and Jonathan
A Widow Shares With Elijah
Elisha's Room on the Roof
Jesus Feeds 5,000
Jesus Make Breakfast for His Friends

Sand and Pencil

Materials
sandpaper
colored pencils
pencil sharpeners

Guide Each Child To
1. Choose colored pencils.
2. Draw a landscape picture on the sandpaper with the pencils.

Talk About
• What would you have seen if you had been in our story when it really happened? Did it happen at the seashore or in a desert? Did it happen on a rocky road?
• What would you have heard if you had been there?
• What would you have smelled if you had been there?
• What did the people do in the story? What did God do?
• What does God do in your life?

Suggested Bible Stories
Abraham and Lot
Israelites Wander in the Wilderness
Jesus Chooses Twelve Friends (the fishermen)
Jesus Stills the Storm
Paul to Damascus

Bookmarks

Materials

bookmark example
paper, any color, cut to 2 by 6 inches
    (one for each child)
assortment of stickers
crayons, markers
clear Contact paper
scissors

Guide Each Child To

1. Decorate the paper, using stickers, crayons, and markers.
2. Help the teacher sandwich the paper between two sheets of clear Contact paper.
3. Cut out his bookmark.

Talk About

• You can use your bookmark to mark a special place in your Bible.
• What does the Bible say?
• What is your favorite Bible story?
• What does the Bible tell us about God?

Suggested Bible Stories

The Ten Commandments
David Plays the Harp (Psalms)
King Josiah Finds God's Word
Jesus as a Boy in the Temple
Jesus Reads in the Synagogue
Philip and the Man From Ethiopia

Secret Message

Materials
plain white paper
blue pencils
red pencils
transparent red plastic theme covers

Guide Each Child To
1. Draw a picture on the paper in blue pencil.
2. Write her name over the picture with red pencil, or draw other parts of the picture with red pencil.
3. Lay the red plastic over the paper. The red part of the drawing will be blocked out and only the blue will show.

Talk About
- Does anyone send you messages? How?
- Who got a message in our story? What was the message?
- What is God's message for us?

Suggested Bible Stories
Jacob and Esau (Jacob returns and Esau forgives him)
Joseph's Brothers Go to Egypt (Joseph forgives his brothers)
Balaam's Talking Donkey
King Josiah Finds God's Word
Rebuilding Jerusalem's Walls
Writing on the Wall
John the Baptist

Night Windows Mural

Materials
butcher paper
rectangular box
crayons, markers

Guide Each Child To
1. Watch as the teacher traces around the box on the butcher paper, making a "window" for each child.
2. Color a nighttime scene in the window as if they are inside looking out. This can become a bulletin board or wall decoration.

Talk About
• What do you see from your window at night?
• What is your bed like? Do you have a night light in your room?
• Who takes care of you at night? How did God take care of the person in our story?

Suggested Bible Stories
Jacob's Dream
Joseph's Dreams
Crossing the Red Sea
Gideon
Samson (taking the gates at night)
Samuel Hears God
David Spares Saul's Life at Night
Jesus Is Born
Nicodemus Visits Jesus at Night
Paul in a Basket

Sand Hand

Materials

sandpaper
crayons
waxed paper
iron, ironing board

Guide Each Child To

1. Let the teacher trace his hand onto his sandpaper.
2. Color his handprint.
3. Watch as the teacher places waxed paper on top of the handprint, then irons to melt the crayon, using short strokes to prevent smearing.

Talk About

• These are your helping hands. How are we helping make a picture?
• Did you ever see anyone help at home by ironing?
• How can you help at home? How can you help at class?
• How did the person in our story help?

Suggested Bible Stories

Isaac Gets a Wife (Rebekah draws water for the camels)
Jacob's Family (Jacob gets water for Rachel's sheep)
Baby Moses (Miriam helps)
Rahab and the Spies
Ruth
Saul Looks For Lost Donkeys
David, the Shepherd Boy
A Widow's Oil Jars
An Ax Head Floats
Through the Roof
The Man's Withered Hand
Woman Touches Jesus' Hem

Handshake Picture

Materials
plain white paper
pencils
crayons, markers

Guide Each Child To
1. Turn her paper horizontally in front of her.
2. Place her right hand on the top right hand side of the paper, fingers together (not spread) pointed to the left and thumb pointing down.
3. Let the teacher draw around her hand.
4. Write her name or let the teacher help her write her name in her handprint.
5. Choose a friend in class to place his right hand on the bottom left hand side of the paper, fingers together pointed to the right and thumb pointing up.
6. Let the teacher draw around the friend's hand.
7. Have the friend write his name in his handprint. It will look like the hands are getting ready to shake hands.

Talk About
- How do friends act toward each other?
- What do you like to do with your friends?
- Who were friends in our story? What happened? Was the friend a good friend or a bad friend?
- Why is it important to choose good friends?

Suggested Bible Stories
David and Jonathan
Elijah Goes to Heaven
Elisha's Room on the Roof
Daniel Refuses the King's Food
The Fiery Furnace
Jesus Chooses Twelve Friends
Through the Roof
Mary and Martha
Paul and Silas in Prison
Paul With Aquila and Priscilla

Paper
Plates
and
Cups

Paper Plate Watermelon

Materials

one paper plate for each child
scissors
red and green crayons
clean, dry watermelon seeds
glue

Guide Each Child To

1. Fold the paper plate in half, open it back up, and cut along the fold. (Some children will need help.)
2. Color the curved edges of his two plate halves green.
3. Color the rest of the plate red.
4. Glue watermelon seeds onto the red part of the plate halves so that they look like watermelon slices.
5. Tell who he will give one of his watermelon slices to.

Talk About

• What's your favorite food? Do you like watermelon?
• Did you ever share your food with someone? Has anyone shared food with you? Tell about it.
• Who shared in our story?

Suggested Bible Stories

Abraham and the Three Visitors
David and Mephibosheth
Ravens Feed Elijah
Elisha's Room on the Roof
Jesus Feeds 5,000
The Lord's Supper

Paper Cup Lions

Materials
one paper cup for each child (not a Styrofoam or
  plastic cup)
crayons, markers
scissors

Guide Each Child To
1. Make a fringe around the top of the cup by cutting slits one-third of the way into the cup from the rim down. Fringe the cup all the way around the rim.
2. Fold the fringes down and out.
3. Turn the cup sideways and draw eyes, nose, and mouth on it.
4. Put her hand into the cup to make the puppet.

Talk About
• What sound does a lion make?
• What is a mother lion called? What are baby lions called?
• Who made lions?
• Tell about the lion(s) in the story.

Suggested Bible Stories
Creation of Animals
Noah (animals)
Samson (kills a lion)
David, the Shepherd Boy
Daniel and the Lions

Paper Plate Animals

Materials
paper plates
tape or stapler
scissors
construction paper
crayons

Guide Each Child To
Make a fish:
1. Cut a triangular pie shape from one side of the paper plate, as shown on page 73. This makes the mouth.
2. Tape or staple the piece that was cut out to the opposite side of the plate to make a tail.
3. Color the fish.

Make a turtle:
1. Cut a rounded head, smaller round feet, and a triangle-shaped tail out of construction paper, as shown on page 73. The upside-down plate becomes the top of the turtle shell.
2. Tape or staple the feet, tail, and head on.
3. Color the turtle.

Make a snail:
1. Cut the snail's head out of construction paper, as shown on page 73.
2. Tape or staple it onto the paper plate as shown. The paper plate is the shell.
3. Color the snail.

Talk About
• Who made animals?
• Where does this animal spend most of its time? How did God make him to be especially able to live there? How does this animal move around? Where does he get his food? How does he sleep?
• Who knows what is best for each animal? Who knows what is best for you?
• What animal was in our story? What did it do?

Suggested Bible Stories
Creation of Animals
Noah (animals)
Balaam's Talking Donkey
Ravens Feed Elijah
Jonah
The Great Catch of Fish
Jesus Feeds 5,000
Tax Money in a Fish
The Fish and the Net
The Triumphal Entry
Jesus Makes Breakfast for His Friends

Hats

Materials
paper plates cut as shown
two 18-inch lengths of thin ribbon or string for each
  child
hole punch
crayons, markers

Guide Each Child To
1. Fold up the flap in the paper plate.
2. Punch one hole in each of two opposite sides of
the plate.
3. Color the plate to be a band leader's hat.
4. Help tie string or ribbon through the holes to
keep the hat on his head.

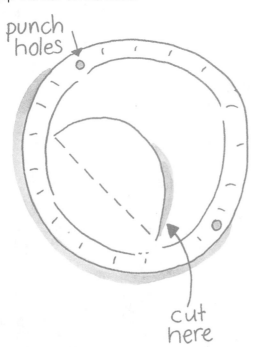

punch
holes

cut
here

Talk About
• Which is best: trying to do things with a
leader or without a leader?
• Who was the leader in this activity? Who is
the leader at home? Who is your leader at
your church? At school? When you play with
your friends?
• Who is the best leader of everyone?

Suggested Bible Stories
Joseph Leads Egypt
Crossing the Red Sea (Moses as leader)
Deborah
Gideon
David Is Anointed
Elijah on Mt. Carmel
Singers Lead Jehoshaphat's Army
Rebuilding Jerusalem's Walls
Esther
John the Baptist
Nicodemus Visits Jesus at Night

Masks

Materials
paper plates
hole punch
string
scissors
crayons, markers
glue
yarn

Guide Each Child To
1. Let the teacher put the paper plate up to the child's face and mark a small X on the plate over the area where his eyes are.
2. Let the teacher cut circles in the plate around the X to make the eye holes.
3. Color the face of the person he chooses from the story. (Or he could choose to make the face of an animal in the story.)
4. Glue yarn on the plate for hair.
5. Help the teacher punch one hole in each side of the plate in line with the eye holes.
6. Let the teacher tie the string in each hole.
7. Put the mask on and act out the story.

Talk About
• Who were some of the people or animals in the story? What did they do? What do you think they might have looked like?
• God had a special plan for them. Did they do what God wanted?
• Do you think God has a special plan for you?

Suggested Bible Stories
Noah (animals)
Abraham and the Three Visitors
Joseph's Brothers Go to Egypt
Twelve Spies
Samson
Ruth
David and Goliath
David and Jonathan
Solomon
Daniel and the Lions
The Wise Men
Jesus Chooses the Twelve Friends
Nicodemus Visits Jesus at Night
Mary and Martha
Peter and Cornelius
Paul and Silas in Prison

Joy Mosaic

Materials
paper plate with the word JOY written on it in block
    letters, one plate for each child
food stickers

Guide Each Child To
1. Share a sheet of food stickers with another
child.
2. Put stickers inside the block letters.
3. Use more stickers as needed.

Talk About
• This spells *joy*. What makes people joyful or
happy? How do people feel when you share
with them?
• Who shared in our story? What did they
share?

Suggested Bible Stories
Abraham and the Three Visitors
David and Jonathan
A Widow Shares With Elijah
Jesus Feeds 5,000
Jesus Makes Breakfast for His Friends

Prayer Reminder

Materials

large Styrofoam cups
pencil
scissors
ribbon or yarn
crayons, markers

Guide Each Child To

1. Place his hand on the side of his cup, fingers facing the bottom.
2. Let the teacher trace around his hand.
3. Let the teacher cut out the handprint, being careful not to cut through the border ring around the rim of the cup and leaving the hand attached to the border.
4. Stand the handprint up, with the border ring as the base.
5. Tie a piece of ribbon or yarn around one of the fingers.
6. Write or let the teacher help him write "Pray" around the border.
7. Color the hand.

Talk About
• Why do we pray? When can we pray? Where can we pray?
• God listens to our prayers. Who prayed in our story? Did God answer the prayer?
• What would you like to talk to God about now?

Suggested Bible Stories

Crossing the Red Sea
Hannah Prays for a Baby
Daniel and the Lions
Jonah
The Lord's Prayer
A Pharisee and a Tax Collector Pray
Paul and Silas in Prison

Paper Wreath

Materials

paper plates with the center cut out, making a
   wreath shape
variety of leaves
glue
self-stick gift wrap bows

Guide Each Child To

1. Glue leaves on her wreath.
2. Select a gift wrap bow.
3. Stick it on the wreath.

Talk About

• This wreath is made of leaves. What do leaves make you think of?
• What color are leaves during the summer? What color are some leaves in the fall or autumn?
• Who made plants? Do you have plants in your yard or in your house?
• Tell about the plants in our story. What happened?

Suggested Bible Stories

Creation of Plants
Garden of Eden
Birds and Flowers (Sermon on the Mount)
The Resurrection (garden tomb)

Cup Family

Materials
large and small Styrofoam cups
tiny bathroom paper cups
crayons, markers

Guide Each Child To
1. Choose three or four cups to use to make a family.
2. Draw a face on each cup with crayon or marker.
3. Make a family of cups, using the tiny cups for the babies.

Talk About
• Name some people who might be in a family.
• Who is in your family?
• Who planned for us to be in families?
• Who was in a family in our story?

Suggested Bible Stories
Adam and Eve Have a Family
Isaac Is Born
Jacob and Esau
Joseph's Brothers Go to Egypt
Rahab and the Spies (Rahab saves her family)
Ruth (Ruth and Boaz have a baby)
David Is Anointed (Jesse and sons)

Boats

Materials
paper plates
crayons, markers

Guide Each Child To
1. Fold the paper plate in half.
2. Color the outsides of the "boat."
3. Set the boat on its rounded edges and rock it back and forth.

Talk About
• Have you ever ridden in a boat? What was it like?
• Who rode in a boat in our story? What happened?
• Who was taking care of the people in our story?
• How does God take care of you?

Suggested Bible Stories
Noah (boats)
Jonah
The Great Catch of Fish
Jesus Stills the Storm
Jesus Walks on Water
Paul's Shipwreck

Design a Coin

Materials
small Styrofoam plates
aluminum foil
pencils

Guide Each Child To
1. Cover the plate with foil.
2. Turn the plate upside down on the table.
3. Draw a design on the foil, using a pencil.

Talk About
- What do we use money for?
- Does money make you happy?
- Who gives us the money we use? How do we get money?
- Who had money in our story? What happened?

Suggested Bible Stories
Joseph's Brothers Go to Egypt (to buy grain)
Solomon
Tax Money in a Fish
The Lost Coin
The Widow's Mite

Goblets

Materials
small, paper bathroom cups
medium or large Styrofoam cups
crayons, markers
glue

Guide Each Child To
1. Color the cups.
2. Turn the small cup upside down, putting glue on the flat end.
3. Place the larger cup's end on top of the glue so that the two cups are now glued together, end-to-end.
4. Allow the glue to dry.

Options: You may cover the bottom half with foil, once the glue has dried. You may wish to glue some "jewels" or buttons on the top cup to make it look more fitting for an Esther feast or for Daniel refusing to eat the king's food.

Talk About
• Who was drinking out of a fancy cup?
• What kind of cups do you drink from?
• Did you ever get really thirsty? What do you like best to drink?
• Who gives us things to drink?

Suggested Bible Stories
Solomon
Nehemiah, the King's Cupbearer
Esther
Daniel Refuses the King's Food
Writing on the Wall

Cup Angels

Materials

Styrofoam cups (each with a small hole poked through the bottom and two vertical slits, one on each side, as shown)
plain white paper
2-foot lengths of string or thread with a button or twist-tie anchored at one end

Guide Each Child To

1. Color a piece of plain white paper.
2. Fold the paper from top to bottom accordion-style (like a fan).
3. Slip the folded paper through the slits in the cup and fan out each side to make wings.
4. Color a face on the front of the cup.
5. Thread the string through the hole in the cup bottom until it is stopped by its "anchor." Hang up the angel.

Suggested Bible Stories
Adam and Eve Leave the Garden
Jacob's Dream
Balaam's Talking Donkey
Samson (an angel tells of Samson's birth)
Daniel and the Lions
Gabriel Appears to Mary
John the Baptist Is Born
Angels Appear to the Shepherds
Joseph, Mary, and Jesus Move to Egypt
The Resurrection (angels at the empty tomb)
Jesus Goes Back to Heaven
Peter Escapes From Prison

Paper Plate Lions

Materials
paper plates
black construction paper
scissors
crayons, markers
glue

Guide Each Child To
1. Cut a black triangle for the nose of the lion and glue it in the center of the plate.
2. Draw eyes or glue on brown paper circles for eyes.
3. Color gold or brown around the bumpy rim of the plate as a mane.
4. Fringe the edges with scissors.
5. Cut thin strips of black paper for whiskers.
6. Gently curl the whiskers by rolling them around a pencil, holding for a moment, and then sliding out the pencil.
7. Glue the whiskers on the plate.

Talk About
• Who saw a lion in our story? What happened?
• How would you have felt if you were in that story?
• What makes you afraid? Who takes care of you when you're afraid?

Suggested Bible Stories
Creation of Animals
Noah (animals)
Samson (kills a lion)
David, the Shepherd Boy
Daniel and the Lions

Plate Angels

Materials
paper plates (cut as shown on page 86)
crayons, markers
hole punch
string

Guide Each Child To
1. Color the angel.
2. Bend the angel's wings back.
3. Punch a hole in the top center of the angel.
4. Tie a string through the hole so he can make the angel fly and hang from the ceiling.

Talk About
• What is an angel?
• Who saw an angel in our story?
• What message did the angel bring from God?
• What message do you think God wants to tell you? How can God tell you his message?

Suggested Bible Stories
Adam and Eve Leave the Garden
Jacob's Dream
Balaam's Talking Donkey
Samson (an angel tells of Samson's birth)
Daniel and the Lions
Gabriel Appears to Mary
John the Baptist Is Born
Angels Appear to the Shepherds
The Resurrection (angels at the empty tomb)
Peter Escapes From Prison

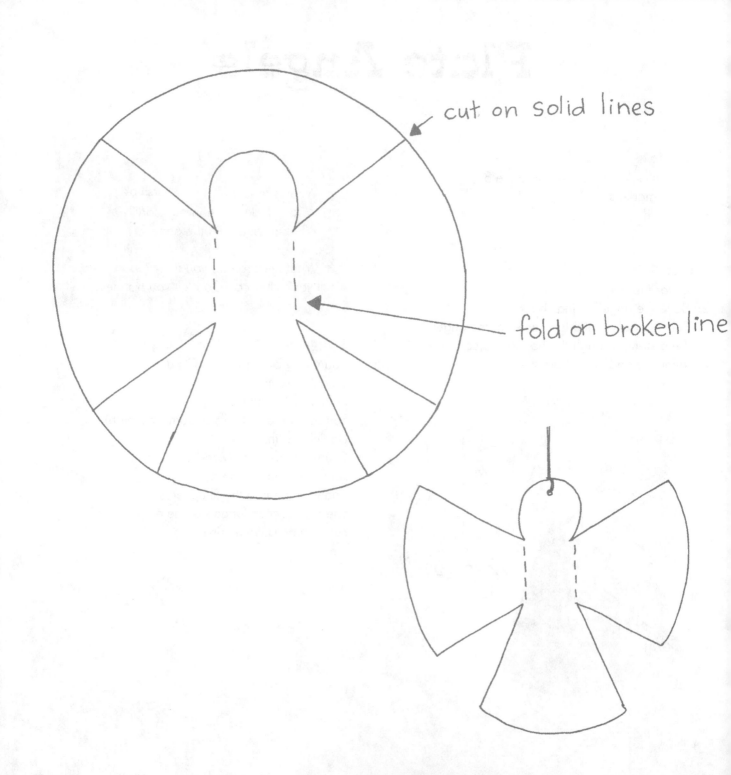

cut on solid lines

fold on broken line

Tambourines

Materials
thick paper plates with three holes punched through one side along the rim, about 3 inches apart (one plate per child)
paper clips, about twelve per child

Guide Each Child To
1. Loop a paper clip through each hole so it dangles from the rim.
2. Link at least three more clips onto each clip in the plate so there are three dangling chains of clips.
3. Color the plates, if desired.
4. Hold the plate by the unclipped side with one hand and strike the plate with the palm of the other, making the tambourine rattle.
5. Sing praise songs accompanied by her tambourine.

Talk About
• What is praise? What is worship? Why is it important?
• How can we praise God with our voices? With our hands? With our feet? With instruments?
• Who praised God in our story?

Suggested Bible Stories
Crossing the Red Sea (Miriam's song of praise)
Deborah (after the battle)
David Plays the Harp (and writes psalms)
Solomon (dedication of the temple)
Singers Lead Jehoshaphat's Army
Gabriel Appears to Mary (Mary's song of praise)
The Triumphal Entry
Children Praise Jesus in the Temple

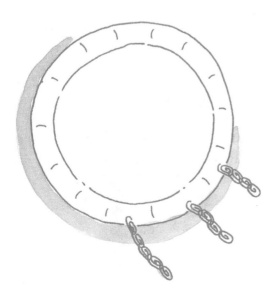

Umbrellas

Materials
paper plates
rubber bands
drinking straws
markers
hole punch

Guide Each Child To
1. Print *Jesus* with marker on the bottom of a paper plate.
2. Twist a rubber band around a drinking straw, about 1 inch from the end.
3. Let the teacher punch a hole in the center of the paper plate.
4. Insert the straw, letting the plate rest on the rubber band.
5. Twist another rubber band onto the straw above the plate. This makes an umbrella.

Talk About
• An umbrella is for protection. What does an umbrella protect you from?
• Name some other things that protect us. How does God protect us?
• How did God protect the people in our story?

Suggested Bible Stories
Noah (weather)
Jonah (weather)
The Wise Man's House
Jesus Stills the Storm
Jesus Walks on Water
Paul's Shipwreck

Cup Chariots

Materials
Styrofoam cups, three for each child
scissors
paper fasteners (brads)

Guide Each Child To
1. Help the teacher cut out the bottom circles from two of the cups.
2. Help the teacher cut the third cup in half, lengthwise.
3. Use one of the halves lying sideways as the chariot.
4. Using the paper fasteners, attach a circle to each side of the chariot as wheels.

Talk About
- What is a chariot?
- Who rode in a chariot in our story?
- How do you travel on a trip?
- Who takes care of you when you travel?

Suggested Bible Stories
Deborah
Elijah Goes to Heaven
Naaman
Servant Sees God's Army
Philip and the Man From Ethiopia

cut off bottoms of two cups

cut another cup in half

attach bottoms of 2 cups to the one half cup with brads

Cup Sheep

Materials
paper or Styrofoam cups
glue or tape
white or black construction paper
scissors
crayons, markers
cotton balls
craft eyes (optional)

Guide Each Child To
1. Cut two ears out of construction paper.
2. Tape or glue the ears on the side of the cup toward the rim, as shown.
3. Cut a triangle nose out of construction paper and glue on the bottom of the cup. Or use a crayon or marker and draw a nose.
4. Draw eyes on the sides or glue on paper circles or craft eyes.
5. Glue cotton balls on the outside area of the cup without covering the eyes or nose.
6. Insert his hand in the cup to use the puppet.

Talk About
• Who took care of sheep in our story? What happened?
• Who takes care of you?
• Do you have animals at home? What do you do to take care of them?

Suggested Bible Stories
Creation of Animals
Noah (animals)
Burning Bush
David, the Shepherd Boy
David Plays the Harp (Psalm 23)
Angels Appears to the Shepherds
The Lost Sheep

Rainbows

Materials
large paper plates cut in half
crayons
hole punch
string

Guide Each Child To
1. Turn his half of the plate so that the curved edge is facing away from him to form the arc of a rainbow.
2. Color the plate with curving stripes of different colors to make a rainbow.
3. Punch a hole in the center of the top of the rainbow.
4. Put the end of a string through the hole in the rainbow and tie it so the rainbow can hang from the ceiling.

Talk About
• Have you ever seen a real rainbow? What was it like?
• Who makes rainbows?
• Where do you like to be when it rains?
• Who takes care of you when it rains or when it's stormy?
• What other kinds of storms are there? Who takes care of you in a storm?
• What's your favorite kind of weather?

Suggested Bible Stories
Noah (rainbows)
Jesus Stills the Storm
Jesus Walks on Water
Paul's Shipwreck

Flying Goose

Materials
paper plates
scissors
string or ribbon
pencil
hole punch

Guide Each Child To
1. Color the top and bottom of the paper plate.
2. Fold the paper plate in half.
3. Help the teacher cut out two triangles, one from each edge, as shown.
4. Punch two holes in the center of the fold, about 1 inch apart, as shown.
5. Fold the wings up.
6. Thread string or ribbon through the holes to hang and fly the goose.

Talk About
• Who made geese?
• What other animals fly?
• What kind of bird was in our story? What did it do?

Suggested Bible Stories
Creation of Animals
Noah (sends the bird out of the ark)
Ravens Feed Elijah
Jesus Is Baptized
Birds and Flowers (Sermon on the Mount)

1.

2.

3.

4.

5.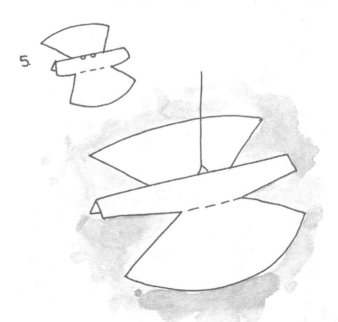

Puppets

Puppet Stage

Materials
light colored fabric, about 40 by 40 inches
four narrow ribbons, 10 inches long
pinking shears
fabric paint
paper plates
tension curtain rod to fit a 30-to-34-inch wide
    window
old newspapers
wet wipes or soap, water and paper towels
    (for clean-up)

Guide Each Child To
1. Help the teacher cut around the raw edges of the fabric with pinking shears.
2. Help the teacher cut eight holes, evenly spaced across the fabric 1 inch from the top. Cut eight holes directly below the others, 4 inches from the top.
3. Fold the top of the fabric over so that the holes match.
4. Thread the ribbons through upper and lower holes to the back of the fabric, then back through the top. Tie the ends of each ribbon together to make a bow. Thread and tie each pair of holes together all the way across.
5. Spread old newspaper on the table or floor.
6. Place the fabric, top side up, on the newspapers.
7. Cover the bottom of the paper plates with paint, one color of paint for each plate.
8. Press a hand into the paint and then onto the fabric.
9. Clean off his hand.
10. Insert the curtain rod into the casing at the top.
11. Place the curtain rod in a door frame or between two shelves or heavy chairs to make a puppet stage.

Talk About
- Who made your hands?
- How do you help with your hands?
- How did the person in our story help? What did the person in our story do with his (hands?

Suggested Bible Stories
Creation of People
The Man's Withered Hand
Woman Touches Jesus' Hem

Paper Bag Puppet

Materials
small paper bags
crayons, markers
string, yarn, or ribbon
glue
colored paper

Guide Each Child To
1. Draw eyes on the paper bag (under the end, a pair of open eyes, and on the end, a pair of closed eyes, as shown, so the puppet can open and close its eyes).
2. Color and glue materials to the paper bag to make hair, a collar, and other features. (The bag is worn over the hand. The eyes open and close with the child's fingers.)

Talk About
• Who do we talk to when we pray? What do we say when we pray? When can we pray? Who can pray? Who prayed in our story? What happened?
• Have you ever had dreams? When do we dream? Who dreamed in our story? What was his dream? What did the dream mean?

Suggested Bible Stories
Prayer:
Hannah Prays for a Baby
Daniel and the Lions
Jonah
The Lord's Prayer
A Pharisee and a Tax Collector Pray
Paul and Silas in Prison

Dreams:
Jacob's Dream
Joseph's Dreams
Baker, Cupbearer, and Pharaoh's Dreams

Finger Puppet

Materials
stiff paper or light cardboard cut from the pattern,
   as shown on page 97
scissors
crayons, markers

Guide Each Child To
1. Color in the features of the puppet.
2. Put her fingers in the holes to make the puppet's legs.

Talk About
• On this puppet, what do your fingers make? How can your puppet move on its legs?
• Who walked in our story? Where did he go?

Suggested Bible Stories
Adam and Eve Leave the Garden
Abraham and the Three Visitors
Crossing the Red Sea
Twelve Spies
The Israelites Wander in the Wilderness
Jericho's Walls Fall Down
Through the Roof
Jesus Walks on Water
The Lame Man at the Pool
The Good Samaritan
The Runaway Son
Peter and John Heal a Lame Man
Philip and the Man From Ethiopia
Paul to Damascus

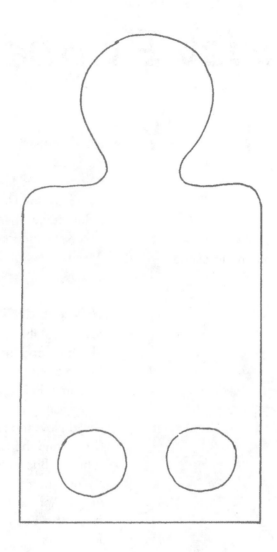

Fist Puppet

Materials
water soluble markers

Guide Each Child To
1. Make a fist.
2. Paint a face on the part of the fist where the thumb is. The area between thumb and forefinger becomes the mouth.

Talk About
• Who made your mouth? What can your mouth do? Does everyone speak the same language?
• Did someone in our story speak some words that are very important to remember?

Suggested Bible Stories
Tower of Babel
Abraham and the Three Visitors (Sarah laughed)
Twelve Spies
Balaam's Talking Donkey (paint a donkey on the fist)
David Plays the Harp (singing)
Daniel and the Lions (paint a lion on the fist)
John the Baptist Is Born (an angel appears to Zechariah)
Angels Appear to the Shepherds
Jesus as a Boy in the Temple
Ten Lepers

Cup Puppet

Materials
Styrofoam cups
yarn
glue
buttons
crayons, markers
fabric scraps and/or cotton balls or cotton batting

Guide Each Child To
1. Turn the cup upside down and glue on yarn for hair.
2. Glue on buttons for eyes or use markers to draw features.
3. Glue on a beard, if he wants.
4. Glue on any other accessories or decoration, as desired.
5. Put his hand into the cup and act out the story.

Talk About
• Who was in our story? What happened?
• Did the person in our story obey God or disobey God?
• Did the person in our story choose to do right?
• What can you do to obey God?

Suggested Bible Story
any Bible story

Spoon Puppet

Materials
plastic spoons
permanent markers
chenille wires
yarn or fabric scraps and glue (optional)

Guide Each Child To
1. Draw a face on the bowl of the spoon.
2. Twist a chenille wire around the handle of the spoon, just under the bowl, as shown. These are the arms.
3. Glue on yarn hair and clothing from fabric scraps, if desired.

Talk About
• Who were the people in our story?
• Did the people in our story obey God or disobey God? What happened?
• What can you do to obey God?

Suggested Bible Story
any Bible story

Double Plate Puppet

Materials

two large paper plates, stapled together facing
each other, leaving a space at one side for a
hand to fit in (one per child)
crayons, markers

Guide Each Child To

1. Draw a smiling face on one side and a frowning
face on the other.
2. Place her hand inside the puppet and act out a
character from the story.

Talk About
• What made the person in the story sad?
What did he do about it? Who saw him?
What made him happy?
• What makes you sad? What makes you
happy? Does God love you when you're sad?
Does God love you when you're happy?

Suggested Bible Stories
Crossing the Red Sea
Hannah Prays for a Son
David Plays the Harp (to sooth King Saul)
A Widow's Oil Jars
Naaman
Through the Roof
The Lame Man at the Pool
The Centurion's Sick Servant
Woman Touches Jesus' Hem
Ten Lepers
Jesus Heals the Bent Woman
Blind Bartimaeus
Hidden Treasures
The Lost Sheep
The Lost Coin
The Runaway Son
Peter and John Heal a Lame Man

Single Plate Puppet

Materials
small paper plates
drinking straws or craft sticks
crayons, markers
tape

Guide Each Child To
1. Draw a face (animal faces or people faces) on the paper plate with the curved side of the plate up.
2. Turn the plate over and tape a drinking straw or craft stick on back.
3. Holding the straw or stick, use the puppet to act out the story.

Talk About
For animal puppets:
• What kinds of animals were in our story? What happened?
• What kind of animal is your favorite?
• Who made animals?

For people puppets:
• Did the person in our story choose to do right or wrong? What happened?
• Tell about a time when you chose to do right or a time when you obeyed.
• Who does God want us to obey?

Suggested Bible Stories
For animal puppets:
Creation of Animals
Noah (animals)
Balaam's Talking Donkey
Jesus Is Born
Angels Appear to the Shepherds

For people puppets:
any story that has people characters

Sun Puppet

Materials
sun shapes cut out of white poster board or
   manila paper
tape
drinking straws
crayons, markers

Guide Each Child To
1. Color the sun shape.
2. Tape it to the top of the straw.

Talk About
• Who made the sun? Where does the sun
go at night?
• What do we call the time of day when the
sun comes up? What do we call the time of
day when the sun goes down?

Suggested Bible Stories
Creation of Sun, Moon, and Stars
Joseph's Dreams
The Sun Stands Still
Let Your Light Shine (Sermon on the Mount)
John Sees Heaven

Bird Puppet

Materials
birds cut out of plain white paper as shown on
    page 105 (one bird for each child)
crayons, markers
tape
drinking straws

Guide Each Child To
1. Color the bird.
2. Cut around the bird outline, but not the fold.
3. Tape the body of the bird together and fold the wings out.
4. Tape a drinking straw to the body of the bird, so he can hold the bird up and make its wings flap.

Talk About
• Where do birds live?
• What do they eat? How do they get their food?
• Do you suppose they ever worry? Who takes care of them?
• What did the bird(s) in our story do?

Suggested Bible Stories
Creation of Animals
Noah (sends out raven and dove)
Ravens Feed Elijah
Jesus Is Baptized
Birds and Flowers (Sermon on the Mount)

Two Eyes

Materials
chenille wires cut in 5-inch lengths
two matching buttons for each child
black permanent marker

Guide Each Child To
1. Thread a button onto each end of a chenille wire.
2. Bend the wire in the middle of the space between the two buttons.
3. Place his middle finger in the bend of the chenille wire so the forefinger and ring finger are on the outside of the bend as shown.
4. Close his fingers and slide the buttons down until they touch his hand. Twist the ends of the wire so the buttons stay on to make eyes.
5. Color the twisted ends black with a marker to make pupils for these eyes.
6. Make the puppet talk by moving his thumb and fingers apart and then together again.

Talk About
• Who gave us eyes to see?
• Who was blind in our story? What happened?
• Do you know anyone who is blind? How does God want us to treat people who are blind?
• What kinds of things do you like to see and watch?
• How can you thank God for your eyes?

Suggested Bible Stories
Birthright and Blessing
Blind Bartimaeus
Paul to Damascus

Sock Puppet

Materials
socks
fabric markers
crayons
fluted coffee filters with sections cut out as shown
safety pins

Guide Each Child To
1. Try the sock on her hand, placing her thumb in the heel of the sock.
2. Make two small dots where the eyes should go.
3. Take the puppet off her hand and draw the eyes in place with fabric markers.
4. Color the coffee filter to be hair. (The filter can be cut shorter or fringed, if the child wants to vary the hairstyle. For Samson, leave the hair long.)
5. Pin the hair on the puppet.

To make an angel:
Color the coffee filter to make angel wings.
Pin the wings on the sock just above the wrist.

Talk About
• Did the person in our story obey or disobey God? What happened?
• Who saw the angel in the story? What happened?
• How can you obey God?

Suggested Bible Stories
Balaam's Talking Donkey
Samson
Gabriel Appears to Mary
John the Baptist Is Born (Zechariah sees an angel)
Angels Appear to the Shepherds
The Resurrection (angels at the empty tomb)
Peter Escapes from Prison

hair

angel wings

Felt Hand Puppet

Materials
two felt mitten shapes per child, cut as shown on
    page 109
glue
permanent marker
yarn, buttons, fabric scraps

Guide Each Child To
1. Draw a smiling face on the piece of felt
(where fingers would be if it were a mitten).
2. Decorate the puppet with yarn hair, buttons or
scraps of fabric for vests, scarves, and other
clothing.
3. Glue along the outside edge of the second
mitten piece, being careful not to glue the opening
for his hand.
4. Lay the decorated mitten half on top of the
glued mitten piece. Let it dry.

Talk About
• *Serving* is another word for *helping*. How
did the person in our story serve? In other
words, how did he help?
• How can you serve and help others?

Suggested Bible Stories
Baby Moses (Miriam helps)
Ruth
Saul Looks for Lost Donkeys
A Widow's Oil Jars
Elisha's Room on the Roof
Naaman (the servant girl helps)
Peter's Mother-in-Law
Jesus Feeds 5,000
Let Your Light Shine (Sermon on the Mount)
Two Sons and a Vineyard

Cloth Angel

Materials

squares of soft cloth (bandanna or handkerchief size), one for each child
gift wrapping ribbon
scissors

Guide Each Child To

1. Lay the cloth flat in front of him.
2. Roll the right and left sides toward each other to meet in the middle like a scroll.
3. Fold the top of the scroll down halfway, rolled side to rolled side. (He is working on the back of the angel.)
4. Help the teacher tie the angel 1 or 2 inches from the fold with gift wrap ribbon to make a head. (The short rolls are arms, the long rolls are legs.)
5. Help the teacher pull the fabric between the short rolls up and over the "head" to make wings.
6. Turn the angel over to see the front.
7. Draw eyes and mouth if he wants.

Talk About

• Who saw the angel in our story?
• How did that person feel? How would you have felt?
• What message did the angel bring?
• What message does God tell you in his word, the Bible?
• How can you tell that message to other people?

Suggested Bible Stories

Adam and Eve Leave the Garden
Jacob's Dream
Balaam's Talking Donkey
Samson (an angel tells of Samson's birth)
Daniel and the Lions
Gabriel Appears to Mary
John the Baptist Is Born
Angels Appear to the Shepherds
Joseph, Mary, and Jesus Move to Egypt
The Resurrection (angels at the empty tomb)
Jesus Goes Back to Heaven
Peter Escapes from Prison

roll sides in

fold top down and tie string tightly

turn over

bring back section up and over head

Clothespin Puppet

Materials
spring-type clothespins
modeling dough (see recipes, pages 116-121)
glue
sharp point permanent marker
cotton balls
yarn

Guide Each Child To
1. Take a small ball of modeling dough.
2. Lay the clothespin on a flat side.
3. Put a dot of glue about ½ to ¾ inch away from the spring end.
4. Gently press the ball of dough onto the dot of glue and mold it to be rounded for a people puppet or mold it to have two points for ears for an animal puppet.
5. Help make two eyes on the dough with the marker.

Optional: Glue yarn hair onto the puppet, or gently stretch a cotton ball and glue it on for hair. Part of a cotton ball can also be glued on for a beard. To make the puppet talk, open and close the clothespin.

play dough molded around and glued

Talk About
• Who gave us mouths to talk?
• What are some kind things we can say?
• What can we say to praise and thank God with our mouths?
• What kind things did the person in our story say (or what did the person in our story say to praise and thank God)?
• What can you say to praise and thank God?

Suggested Bible Stories
Tower of Babel
Joseph's Brothers Go to Egypt (Joseph forgives them)
Balaam's Talking Donkey
Ruth
Hannah Prays for a Baby
David and Jonathan
David and Mephibosheth
Singers Lead Jehoshaphat's Army
Ten Lepers
Jesus and the Children
The Triumphal Entry

Box Puppet

Materials

empty cereal or rice boxes (cut as shown)
stapler
index cards
crayons, markers

Guide Each Child To
1. Color the features on the puppet.
2. Help staple an index card on the back as shown, slipping her hand under the index card to hold up the figure.

Note: If you use a small, single serving cereal box, cut the index card to fit the puppet, and use it as a finger puppet.

Talk About
• Did the person in our story make the right choices? Did he obey or disobey God?
• How do you know how to act? How do you know the right thing to choose?
• What does God want you to do?

Suggested Bible Story
any Bible story

1.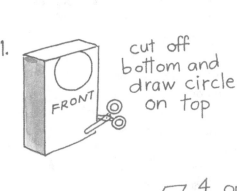
cut off bottom and draw circle on top
FRONT

2. cut down sides and out around circle

3. cut out V-shape in back
back

4. open flat and attach index card

5. stick hand under index card to hold puppet up
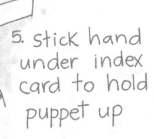

Plastic Bag Puppet

Materials
plastic sandwich bags
permanent markers

Guide Each Child To
1. Place the sandwich bag flat on the table with the opening toward him.
2. Draw a face on the top half of the sandwich bag.
3. Put his hand in the sandwich bag with the face on the palm side of his hand.
4. Punch holes below and to the side of the face with his little finger and thumb.
5. Stick his little finger and thumb through the holes to make arms for the puppet.
6. Help act out the story with his puppet.

Talk About
• Who was sick in our story? What happened?
• Who is the one who can make us well when we are sick?
• Tell about a time when you were sick. Who took care of you?
• When someone else is sick, what can we do for them?

Suggested Bible Stories
Naaman
King Hezekiah Gets Well
Peter's Mother-in-Law
Through the Roof
The Man's Withered Hand
Jairus's Daughter
Jesus Heals the Bent Woman
Peter and John Heal a Lame Man

Bottle Cap Puppet

Materials
plastic screw-on bottle caps
modeling dough (see recipes, pages 116-121)
fine-tip permanent markers
small squares of fabric, yarn, glue (optional)

Guide Each Child To
1. Put a ball of modeling dough inside the bottle cap.
2. Push her forefinger into the dough to make a hole that fits her finger.
3. Draw a face on the side of the bottle cap by herself or with a teacher's help. The top of the puppet's head is the top of the bottle cap.

Optional: Glue yarn on top of the bottle cap to make hair, or glue a small square of fabric on top to make a Bible times head covering. Help act out the story using her puppet.

Talk About
• Who were the people in our story?
• Did they obey or disobey God? What happened?
• How can you obey God?

Suggested Bible Story
any Bible story that has people characters

Modeling Dough

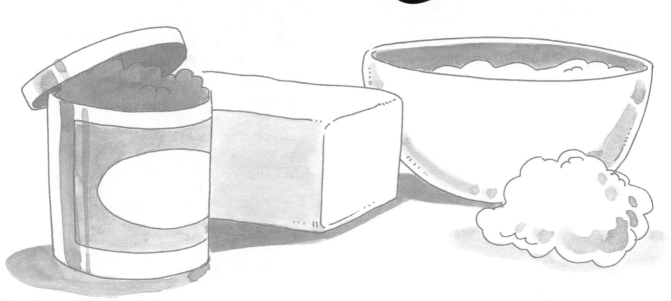

Ooze Dough

with dough recipe

Materials
two parts cornstarch
one part water
big bowl
large paper plates
plastic spoons
food coloring

Guide Each Child To
1. Help mix the cornstarch and water.
2. Pour some of this mixture onto a paper plate.
3. Try molding a figure out of it.
4. Drip one drop of food coloring on the dough and stir or swirl it in with a plastic spoon.
5. Drip a drop of a different color onto the dough and stir or swirl it in.
6. Continue exploring with the ooze dough and the colors. Pretend the dough is a cloud and swirl it around to make a storm.

Talk About
• God makes things out of nothing. We say he creates. Can we make things out of nothing? Can we make people or trees or grass or animals?
• Can you make anything out of ooze dough?
• Who made colors? What happens when you add a new color to the ooze dough?

Suggested Bible Stories
Creation of Sky, Sea, and Land
Noah (rainbows)
The Plagues in Egypt (hail)
The Ten Commandments (cloud on Mt. Sinai)
The Cloud Covers the Tabernacle
Elijah on Mt. Carmel (fire from heaven, servant sees a cloud)
Jonah (weather)
Jesus Stills the Storm
Jesus Walks on Water
Paul's Shipwreck

Salt Dough Face

with dough recipe

Materials
water
salt
flour
large bowl
mixing spoon
garlic press (optional)
waxed paper

Guide Each Child To
1. Help mix 1 part water, 1 part salt, and 3 parts flour.
2. Knead the mixture.
3. Place some of the dough on waxed paper.
4. Use the dough for one of the activities in this section of this book, or make a dough face by the following instructions.
5. Flatten the dough into a round shape like a big pancake.
6. Roll smaller balls of dough and flatten them to make eyes and ears to put on the round dough to make a face.
7. Roll smaller balls of dough and shape them to make a nose and mouth for this face.
8. Press some of the dough in the garlic press to make hair. For Samson, roll out long ropes of dough for the hair.

Talk About
- Who makes people? Who made you?
- Does everyone look alike? How are people different?
- Who were some of the people in our story? What did they do?

Suggested Bible Stories
Creation of People
Jacob and Esau
Samson
David and Jonathan
Jesus Chooses Twelve Friends
Zacchaeus

Cloud Dough Rainbow

with dough recipe

Materials
vegetable oil
flour
water
food coloring
large bowl
mixing spoon
measuring cups
waxed paper

Guide Each Child To
1. Help mix 1 cup of vegetable oil, 6 cups of flour, and 1 cup of water. (Divide the dough into four parts.)
2. Use the dough for one of the activities in this section of this book, or make a dough rainbow by the following instructions.
3. Help mix a different color of food coloring into each part: red, green, yellow, blue.
4. Put a small ball of each color of dough onto his waxed paper.
5. Roll each color of dough into a "snake."
6. Place the snakes of dough side-by-side and curve them into an arch to make a rainbow.

Talk About
- Who puts rainbows in the sky?
- Who saw the first rainbow?
- Have you ever seen a real rainbow? What was it like?
- Who takes care of you when it rains?

Suggested Bible Stories
Noah (rainbow)
Joseph's Colorful Coat

Cornstarch Dough Baby

with dough recipe

Materials
water
salt
cornstarch
stove, hot plate, or microwave
pot to heat mixture in
mixing spoon
paper plate

Guide Each Child To
1. Help heat the water and salt.
2. Slowly add the cornstarch and stir well.
3. Make sure the mixture is not too hot to touch. When it's still warm, knead it.
4. Place some of the dough on a paper plate.
5. Use the dough for one of the activities in this section of this book, or make a dough baby by the following instructions.
6. Divide the dough on the plate into two parts, one larger and one smaller.
7. Roll the larger section of dough into an oval shape to make the baby's body.
8. Roll the smaller section of dough into a ball shape to make the baby's head.
9. Put the oval and the ball together, side-by-side.
10. Roll smaller balls of dough to make eyes, nose, mouth, and ears.

Talk About
• Do you have a baby at your house? If you know a baby, tell what a baby is like.
• Who had a baby in our story? What happened?
• How can you help when you are around a baby?

Suggested Bible Stories
Isaac Is Born
Ruth (Ruth and Boaz have a baby)
Hannah Prays for a Baby
John the Baptist Is Born
Jesus Is Born

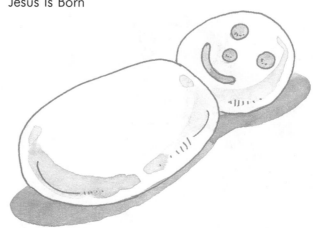

Oatmeal Dough Animal

with dough recipe

Materials
flour
water
oats
raisins
large bowl
mixing spoon
measuring cups
waxed paper

Guide Each Child To
1. Help mix 1 part flour, 2 parts oats, and 1 part water.
2. Put some dough on a piece of waxed paper.
3. Mold the dough into animal shapes. Use raisins for facial features.

Talk About
- What kind of animal are you making?
- What is your favorite animal?
- Who made animals?
- What kind of animal was in our story? What happened?

Suggested Bible Stories
Creation of Animals
Noah (animals)
Balaam's Talking Donkey
David, the Shepherd Boy
Daniel and the Lions
Jesus Is Born
The Triumphal Entry

Poco Clay Fish and Bread

with dough recipe

Materials
peanut butter
powdered milk
honey
oats
coconut
large bowl
mixing spoon
measuring cups
paper plates

Guide Each Child To
1. Help mix equal parts of peanut butter and powdered milk.
2. Add honey until the mixture is thick.
3. Stir in oats and coconut.
4. If the clay is too sticky, add more powdered milk.
5. Mold the dough on a paper plate. Make bun shapes or fish shapes, or use one of the dough activities on the following pages.

Note: This is a dough that children can play with and then eat when they're finished. If you plan to let the children eat their creations, you will need to make sure that their hands are clean before they begin this activity. Also, make sure that they use clean utensils when making designs in the dough.

Talk About
- What did the people in the story eat?
- How did they get their food?
- Who gives us our food?

Suggested Bible Stories
Manna and Quail
Ruth
Abigail Packs Food
Ravens Feed Elijah
A Widow Shares With Elijah
Daniel Refuses the King's Food
John the Baptist (locusts and honey)
Jesus Feeds 5,000
The Lord's Supper
Jesus Makes Breakfast for His Friends

Car Tracks

Materials
modeling dough (see recipes, pages 116-121)
waxed paper
variety of toy cars and trucks

Guide Each Child To
1. Flatten the dough on waxed paper.
2. Roll the toy cars and trucks over the dough to make tracks.

Talk About
• Do you walk to church or do you ride? If you ride, what do you ride in?
• How do you get to your grandmother's house?
• What are some other ways to travel?
• What is your favorite way to travel?
• Who traveled in our story? Where did they go? What happened?

Suggested Bible Stories
Noah
Abraham Travels
The Israelites Wander in the Wilderness
The Wise Men
Joseph, Mary, and Jesus Move to Egypt
Philip and the Man From Ethiopia

Praying Hands

Materials
modeling dough (see recipes, pages 116-121)
waxed paper

Guide Each Child To
1. Make a flat circle of modeling dough.
2. Press her handprint in it with her fingers together so it will resemble praying hands.
3. Let it dry.

Talk About
- What is prayer?
- When can you pray? What can you pray about? Who can you pray to? Where can you pray? Why would you want to pray?
- Who prayed in our story? Why? What happened?

Suggested Bible Stories
Crossing the Red Sea
Hannah Prays for a Baby
Daniel and the Lions
Jonah
The Lord's Prayer
A Pharisee and a Tax Collector Pray
Paul and Silas in Prison

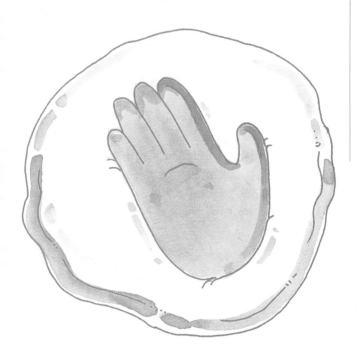

Sole Prints

Materials
modeling dough (see recipes, pages 116-121)
waxed paper
a variety of shoes, different sizes (the soles should
  be fairly clean)

Guide Each Child To
1. Flatten the dough on the waxed paper.
2. Pat the dough with flour if it's too sticky.
3. Gently press the soles of different shoes onto the
dough to reveal the designs on the soles of the
shoes.

Option: Use the children's shoes to make the sole
prints.

Talk About
• Who makes sure that we have clothes to
wear?
• What happens to your clothes as you grow?
• What's your favorite thing to wear?
• What special clothes did the person in our
story have?
• What happened in our story?

Suggested Bible Stories
Adam and Eve Leave the Garden (God makes
  clothes for them)
Joseph's Colorful Coat
Samuel's New Coats
Esther (Mordecai wears the king's robe)
John the Baptist (camel's hair, leather belt)
The Lame Man at the Pool
Peter and John Heal a Lame Man
Dorcas

Manger

Materials
modeling dough (see recipes, pages 116-121)
garlic press
egg cartons cut into individual cups

Guide Each Child To
1. Assist his teacher in squeezing dough through the garlic press to make hay.
2. Place hay in his egg carton cup manger.
3. Make a small baby figure by rolling a small ball for the body and a smaller ball for the head. Put these together and place them in the hay.

Talk About
• Why did Mary put baby Jesus in a manger? What is a manger?
• How would you feel if there were no rooms left in any hotels in a city you were traveling to?
• What kinds of sounds do you think the baby might have heard in the stable? Who came to see him there?

Suggested Bible Story
Jesus Is Born

King's Seal

Materials
modeling dough (see recipes, pages 116-121)
small cans or medicine containers
various sizes of screws

Guide Each Child To
1. Flatten the dough into a small circle.
2. Select cans, medicine containers, and/or screws to stamp designs into her dough.

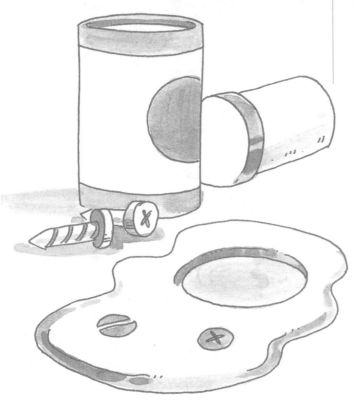

Talk About
• Long ago, kings had special rings they wore. These were called signet rings. When the king sent a message or made a law, he would stamp his own ring into the clay or into wax. That meant that it was from the king.
• Kings also put a seal over the opening of something so they would know if someone had opened it. Did you ever see a seal over the opening of something? What was it? Why was the seal there?
• Who was the king in our story? What did he stamp? Why? Who is our king?

Suggested Bible Stories
Esther
Daniel and the Lions
The Resurrection (tomb no longer sealed)

Wreath Gift

Materials
modeling dough (salt dough, p. 117, will dry hard
   for a keepable wreath)
green food coloring
paper plates
cake decorations:
   red hots
   silver and gold balls
   flowers, leaves
   sprinkles
   heart-shaped Valentine candies
garlic press (optional)

Guide Each Child To
1. Mix the green food coloring into the modeling
dough.
2. Make a "snake" from his dough.
3. Press the ends of the snake together to form a
circle.
4. Decorate the wreath with cake decorations.

Optional: Squeeze some dough through the garlic
press to make fine, leafy tendrils. Cut these off and
gently press them into the wreath.

Talk About
• Who are you going to give your wreath to?
• Who gave something in our story? What
did they give?
• How do you feel when someone gives you
a gift?
• How do you feel when you give someone
else a gift?
• Why does God want us to be cheerful
givers?
• What are some things God has given to
us?

Suggested Bible Stories
Isaac Gets a Wife
Joseph's Colorful Coat
David and Jonathan
Abigail Packs Food
The Wise Men
Perfume on Jesus' Feet

Soap Flake Sea

Materials
Ivory Flakes laundry detergent
water
large mixing bowl
electric mixer
blue food coloring
measuring cup or pitcher
cardboard or stiff paper plates
paper towels

Guide Each Child To
1. Help the teacher gradually add water to the soap flakes while she whips the mixture with the electric mixer.
2. Watch the teacher add drops of blue food coloring when the mixture is thick and creamy.
3. Use this mixture as a finger paint.
4. Paint it on the cardboard or plate, making peaks as if they were waves.
5. Let it dry.

WARNING: This mixture is soap. Do not get it in the eyes or mouth.

Talk About
• Who made water?
• How do we travel in or on water?
• What do we use water for? Where might you find water?
• What kind of water was in our story? What happened?

Suggested Bible Stories
Creation of Sky, Sea, and Land
Noah
Crossing the Red Sea
Naaman
Jonah
Jesus Is Baptized
The Great Catch of Fish
Jesus Stills the Storm
Jesus Walks on the Water
Paul's Shipwreck

Coil Pots

Materials
modeling dough (see recipes, pages 116-121)
waxed paper

Guide Each Child To
1. Flatten a small ball of modeling dough into a circle about 3 inches in diameter.
2. Roll the rest of his modeling dough into one long "snake."
3. Press one end of the snake onto the circle of dough at the edge.
4. Coil the rest of the dough around the edge of the circle and back on top of itself.
5. Continue coiling the snake around until all the dough is coiled up, forming a small pot.

Talk About
• Do you have jars and pots at home? What are they used for?
• Who had a jar or pot in our story? What was in it?
• What happened in the story?

Suggested Bible Stories
Isaac Gets a Wife (Rebekah waters the servant's camels)
A Widow Shares With Elijah
A Widow's Oil Jars
Water Into Wine
The Woman at the Well
Perfume on Jesus' Feet

Start by pressing one end of the snake onto the circle

coil around to make a pot

City Walls

Materials
modeling dough (see recipes, pages 116-121)
waxed paper
index cards
plastic knives
paper plates

Guide Each Child To
1. Flatten her modeling dough on the waxed paper, but not too thin.
2. Place an index card on top of the dough and cut around it with the plastic knife.
3. Cut out four of these card-sized panels.
4. Stand the panels up on the plate at right angles to each other to make four walls.
5. Pinch the corners of the dough together.

Option: Everyone joins their wall panels to make a long wall.

Talk About
- Who lived in the city in our story?
- Why would a city have big walls around it?
- What happened in the city in our story?
- What is your city like?
- Do you ever travel to different cities? Is God there?

Suggested Bible Stories
Rahab and the Spies
Jericho's Walls Fall Down
Rebuilding Jerusalem's Walls
The Triumphal Entry
Paul in a Basket

Footprints

Materials

modeling dough (see recipes, pages 116-121)
waxed paper
two peanut shells for each child (peanuts can still
   be in them)

Guide Each Child To

1. Flatten his modeling dough on the waxed paper,
but not too thin.
2. Gently press the two peanut shells into the
dough to make what appears to be small footprints.
3. Make a track of footprints across the dough.

Talk About
• When you take a walk, where do you like
to go?
• Who made our feet to walk?
• Who walked in our story? Where did they
go?

Suggested Bible Stories
Joseph Is Taken to Egypt
Crossing the Red Sea
The Israelites Wander in the Wilderness
Through the Roof
The Lame Man at the Pool
Jesus Washes His Friends' Feet
Peter and John Heal a Lame Man

Dough Mountains

Materials
modeling dough (see recipes, pages 116-121)
paper plates or cardboard squares about 9 inches
   wide
small rocks, gravel or sand
small twigs and plant stems with small leaves

Guide Each Child To
1. Place some of the modeling dough on her plate
or cardboard.
2. Make mountains out of the dough.
3. Press the rocks, gravel, or sand into the sides of
the mountains.
4. Stick twigs and stems with leaves into the sides
of the mountains to make trees.

Talk About
• Have you ever been to the mountains?
What was it like?
• Who saw mountains in our story? What
happened?
• Who made mountains?

Suggested Bible Stories
Creation of Sky, Sea, and Land
Noah
The Ten Commandments
Elijah on Mount Carmel
The Beatitudes (on a mountain)

Food
Art

Apple Star Stamp

Materials

one apple for every two stamps you wish to make
knife for teacher's use
tempera paint, a variety of colors
one piece of plain paper for each child
paper plates, one for each color of paint
paper towels for clean-up

Guide Each Child To

1. Watch as the teacher cuts four sides off the apple and cuts across the center so that the apple has a top half and a bottom half.
2. Cover the bottom of each paper plate with a different color of paint.
3. Press one half of the apple into the paint and then onto the paper, making a star-shaped blank surrounded by a square of color.
4. Fill the paper with a design made of the apple star prints.

Talk About

- Where do we see other stars?
- What else do you see in the sky?
- Who made the stars? Why?
- Tell about the star(s) in our story.

Suggested Bible Stories

Creation of Sun, Moon, and Stars
God's Promise to Abraham
Jacob's Dream
The Plagues in Egypt (darkness)
The Wise Men

Cookie Necklace

Materials
½ cup softened stick margarine
½ cup shortening
1¼ cups powdered sugar
3 hard-cooked egg yolks
1 teaspoon baking soda
½ teaspoon cream of tartar
½ tablespoon vanilla
2½ cups flour
3 colors of food coloring
18 inches of yarn or string for each child
electric mixer
mixing bowl and spoon
four smaller bowls
fork
aluminum foil
baking sheet
oven
pot holders
plastic drinking straws

Guide Each Child To
1. Preheat the oven to 350 degrees.
2. Mix the butter, shortening, and sugar together until fluffy.
3. Mash the egg yolks with a fork in a small bowl.
4. Mix the egg yolks, soda, cream of tartar, and vanilla with the butter mixture.
5. Help divide the dough into four equal parts. Leave one part plain, but color the other three parts with three different colors of food coloring.
6. Place some dough (one color or several) on a piece of foil. Pat it down to about 1/4-inch thick. Shape it as desired, or cut it with a cookie cutter.
7. Place the foil with the dough on it onto a baking sheet. Bake for 8 to 10 minutes.
8. As soon as the cookies come out of the oven, make a hole in each one with the straws.
9. Let cookies cool completely before threading the yarn or string through the holes. Tie the ends of the string or yarn to make a necklace.

Talk About
• Who wears necklaces?
• Tell about some different necklaces you have seen.
• Who wore (or might have worn) a necklace in our story?
• What's a treasure? Do you think there might be necklaces in a treasure chest?

Suggested Bible Stories
Isaac Gets a Wife
Joseph Leads Egypt
Esther
Writing on the Wall
Hidden Treasures

Jelly Bean Nest

Materials
one piece of construction paper for each child
glue
shredded coconut
yellow food coloring
jelly beans or speckled "bird's egg" candies
mixing bowl and spoon

Guide Each Child To
1. Help put the coconut in the bowl, add some yellow food coloring, and stir.
2. Put glue on the paper to form a bird nest.
3. Sprinkle yellow coconut onto the glue.
4. Glue some jellybeans or candies onto the coconut nest.

Talk About
• Did you ever see a bird's nest? What was it like?
• Tell about other places birds might live.
• Do you have a pet bird, or do you know someone who has a pet bird? What is it like?
• Tell about the bird(s) in our story.

Suggested Bible Stories
Creation of Animals
Noah (animals)
Ravens Feed Elijah
Jesus Is Baptized
Birds and Flowers (Sermon on the Mount)

Grain Collage

Materials
paper plates
wide, shallow box (like a shirt box)
barley
unpopped popcorn kernels
oats
wheat or puffed wheat cereal
rice
glue

Guide Each Child To
1. Spread glue on his paper plate.
2. Place different grains on the glue. Some can be sprinkled on, some can be set into the glue.
3. Gently pour any excess grain from the picture into the box.

Talk About
• Who made grain? What do we use grain for?
• How are these grains different? Which is the smallest? Which is the largest?
• When you eat corn, how does it usually look? When you eat other grains, how do they look?
• Have you ever seen grain growing in the field? What was it like?
• Who had grain in our story? What happened?

Suggested Bible Stories
Joseph's Dreams
Baker, Cupbearer, and Pharaoh's Dreams
   (Pharaoh's dream)
Joseph's Brothers Go to Egypt
Ruth
Bigger Barns

Cone Tree

Materials
pointed ice cream cones (sugar cones)
paper plates or green construction paper
white ready-made frosting
green food coloring
green decorative sugar sprinkles
bowl
mixing spoon
plastic spoons or knives

Guide Each Child To
1. Help mix green food coloring into the white frosting.
2. Turn ice cream cones upside down on the paper plate or green construction paper.
3. Use a plastic spoon or knife to frost the upside down cone to make an evergreen tree.
4. Sprinkle green decorative sugar on the frosted tree.

Talk About
• Who made trees?
• What kinds of trees do you see in your neighborhood?
• What kind of tree do you like best?
• What part of our story had a tree in it? What happened?

Suggested Bible Stories
Creation of Plants
Adam and Eve Eat the Fruit
Burning Bush
Deborah
Zacchaeus

Seashore Scene

Materials
construction paper
crayons
uncooked shell-shaped pasta
sand
bowl
glue
wide, shallow box (like a shirt box)

Guide Each Child To
1. Mix the sand and pasta together in a bowl.
2. Draw a lake on part of her picture.
3. Spread glue on the shore of the lake and across the rest of the paper.
4. Place the picture in the shallow box.
5. Sprinkle the mixture of sand and pasta over the glue.
6. Pick up the paper gently, letting the excess sand fall into the box.

Talk About
• Have you ever been to the beach? What did you do there?
• What might you see at a beach?
• What might you hear at a beach?
• Who was at the seashore in our story? What happened?
• Who takes care of you at the beach? By the lake?

Suggested Bible Stories
Creation of Sky, Sea, and Land
Crossing the Red Sea
Jonah
The Great Catch of Fish
Jesus Stills the Storm
Jesus Walks on Water
Paul's Shipwreck

Rice Glitter

Materials

construction paper
uncooked white rice
uncooked brown rice
glue
wide, shallow box (like a shirt box)
crayons, markers

Guide Each Child To

1. Draw a landscape of land and mountains, on his paper.
2. Draw the outline of clouds in the sky on his landscape picture.
3. Spread glue on the ground, the mountains, and the clouds in his picture.
4. Place his picture in the shallow box.
5. Sprinkle brown rice over the land and mountains, and white rice over the clouds.
6. Shake the excess rice off the picture and into the box.

Talk About

• Who made the land and the sky?
• Have you ever been to the mountains? What was it like?
• What kind of land was in our story? What happened there?
• What are some different kinds of land that God made?
• How do you travel? How did the people in our story travel?
• Who takes care of you wherever you go?

Suggested Bible Stories

Creation of Sky, Sea, and Land
Abraham and Lot
Twelve Spies
The Israelites Wander in the Wilderness
Joseph, Mary, and Jesus Move to Egypt (make pyramids in the picture)
The Good Samaritan

Cracker House

Materials
saltine or graham crackers
ready-made frosting
craft sticks
paper plates
paper towels

Guide Each Child To
1. Dip one edge of a cracker into the frosting. Stick the edge of a second cracker to the frosted edge of the first cracker so the crackers are at right angles, forming a corner.
2. Stand this corner up on the plate, forming two walls of the house.
3. Spread frosting on the outer edges of these two walls.
4. Repeat this procedure with two more crackers, using them as the other walls. Stick the four walls together to make the house.
5. Spread frosting on the upper edges of the walls and place a fifth cracker on top to make a roof.

Talk About
- Who gave us places to live?
- What kind of house was in our story? What happened there?
- Tell about the place where you live. Who lives there with you?

Suggested Bible Stories
Tower of Babel
Rahab and the Spies
Solomon (builds the temple)
Elisha's Room on the Roof
Rebuilding Jerusalem's Walls
Writing on the Wall
Jesus Is Born
Through the Roof
The Wise Man's House

Popcorn Flowers

Materials
construction paper
crayons, markers
popped popcorn
glue
paintbrushes
liquid tempera paint (optional)

Guide Each Child To
1. Draw a stem and leaves on the paper.
2. Glue popcorn at the top of the stem to make a flower.
3. When the glue is dry, gently brush over the popcorn with tempera paint to color the flower.

Talk About
• Who made flowers?
• Tell about the flowers (or garden) in our story.
• What is your favorite kind of flower?
• Tell about a garden that you have or one that you have visited.

Suggested Bible Stories
Creation of Plants
Garden of Eden
Birds and Flowers (Sermon on the Mount)
The Resurrection (the garden tomb)

Popcorn Beard

Materials
paper plates
construction paper
popped popcorn
glue
crayons, markers

Guide Each Child To
1. Trace around the plate to make a circle.
2. Draw eyes, nose, mouth, and ears on the circle to make a face.
3. Glue popcorn on the face to make hair and beard.

Talk About
• Do you know anybody who has a beard? What is it like?
• Why do you think God gave men beards?
• Who was the man in our story?
• What did this man do? Did he love and obey God or not?
• What can you do to obey God?

Suggested Bible Stories
Noah
Abraham and the Three Visitors
Burning Bush
Elijah on Mt. Carmel
John the Baptist Is Born (Zechariah)
Anna and Simeon
Peter and Cornelius

Cereal Caterpillar

Materials
construction paper
crayons, markers
donut-shaped dry breakfast cereal
glue

Guide Each Child To
1. Glue the cereal to the paper in a line to make a caterpillar.
2. Draw grass, twigs, and leaves around the caterpillar.

Talk About
- Who made caterpillars?
- What does a caterpillar become when it grows up?
- What are some ways people change as they grow?
- Tell some ways in which you are growing.
- Who grew in our story?

Suggested Bible Stories
Creation of Animals
Noah (animals)
Samuel's New Coats
Joash, Boy King
Josiah, Boy King
Jesus as a Boy in the Temple
Timothy

Pasta Necklace

Materials
string or narrow ribbon cut in 30-inch lengths
dry pasta (tube or wheel shaped with holes in them)

Guide Each Child To
1. Thread the string or ribbon through the holes in the pasta to make a necklace.
2. Let the teacher tie the ends of the string or ribbon together to fit over the child's head and hang around her neck.

Talk About
• Who wore (or might have worn) a necklace in our story?
• What happened in our story?
• Does someone at your house wear a necklace? Who?
• Sometimes we give necklaces as gifts. What kinds of gifts have you given people?
• Why does God want us to be cheerful givers?
• What kinds of gifts does God give us?

Suggested Bible Stories
Isaac Gets a Wife
Joseph Leads Egypt
Queen of Sheba
Esther
Writing on the Wall

Cereal Jewelry

Materials
string (12-inch lengths for bracelets, 30-inch lengths for necklaces)
dry, donut-shaped breakfast cereal

Guide Each Child To
1. Thread the string through the holes in the cereal to make a bracelet or necklace.
2. Let the teacher tie the ends of the string together to fit the child's wrist, leaving the bracelet loose enough to pull it off easily.

Talk About
• Who wore a necklace or bracelet in our story?
• Who gave the necklace (or bracelet) to him?
• Why do people give gifts to other people?
• Sometimes people give necklaces (or bracelets) as gifts. What kinds of gifts have you given to people?
• What gifts has God given us?
• What does it mean to be generous? Why does God want us to be cheerful givers?

Suggested Bible Stories
Isaac Gets a Wife
Joseph Leads Egypt
Writing on the Wall

Pasta People

Materials
construction paper
crayons
dry pasta in a variety of shapes
glue

Guide Each Child To
1. Draw a person on his paper.
2. Glue different shapes of pasta on his figure to make clothes, hair, arms, legs, feet, and so on.

Talk About
• Who made people?
• Who were the people in our story? What happened?
• Tell some ways in which people look different.
• Sometimes we decide what a person is like by looking at the outside. What does God look at?
• How are you like other people in your family? How are you different?

Suggested Bible Stories
Creation of People
Jacob and Esau
Samson
David Is Anointed
Jesus Chooses Twelve Friends
The Woman at the Well
Zacchaeus
Peter and Cornelius

Mosaic Sunshine

Materials
cardboard or poster board, about 8½ by 11 inches
crayon
glue
unpopped popcorn kernels

Guide Each Child To
1. Draw an outline of a sun or star on the cardboard or poster board.
2. Glue the kernels of dried corn inside the outline to make a mosaic.

Talk About
• Who made the sun and stars?
• What else did God make that is in the sky?
• Where is the sun at night? Where are the stars in the daytime?
• Where is the sun on a cloudy, rainy day?
• Why do you think God made the sun (or stars) for us?
• Tell about the sun (or stars) in our story.

Suggested Bible Stories
Creation of Sun, Moon, and Stars
Jacob's Dream
Joseph's Dreams
The Sun Stands Still
The Wise Men
Let Your Light Shine (Sermon on the Mount)
John Sees Heaven

Cracker Altar

Materials
picture of an altar (check a pictorial Bible dictionary)
construction paper
glue
square or rectangular crackers
red, yellow, and orange crayons

Guide Each Child To
1. Look at the picture of an altar. (Explain that it was a place where people put special kinds of gifts they were giving to God, usually meat of some kind. It was a way they worshiped God.)
2. Glue the crackers onto the paper to form an altar shape.
3. Color fire on top of the altar.

Talk About
• What is worship?
• A long time ago, people worshiped by giving God gifts on an altar. Do we worship that way now?
• How do we worship God now?
• Who worshiped God in our story?

Suggested Bible Stories
Noah (after the flood)
Crossing the Jordan
Solomon (dedicates the temple)
Elijah on Mt. Carmel
John the Baptist Is Born (Zechariah in the temple)

Fish Cracker Picture

Materials
light blue construction paper
dark blue crayons
waxed paper scalloped to look like waves
iron, ironing board
stapler
fish-shaped crackers
glue

Guide Each Child To
1. Color dark blue water on the construction paper.
2. Place the waxed paper on top of the crayon water.
3. Place her hand on top of the teacher's hand to help quickly iron over the waxed paper. (Use caution when using the hot iron. Make sure an adult is always supervising and that children stay away from it.)
4. Staple the sides of the waxed paper to the paper to secure it.
5. Glue fish-shaped crackers on top of the waxed paper sea.

Talk About
• Who made fish? What are they like?
• Did you ever go fishing? What did you catch?
• Tell about the fish in our story. What happened?

Suggested Bible Stories
Creation of Animals
The Great Catch of Fish
Jesus Feeds 5,000
Tax Money in a Fish
Jesus Makes Breakfast for His Friends

1.
2.
3.
4.
5.

Index

Index

Index

Index

Index

Index

Index